A CHIZONA RÉSUMÉ

BACKSTAGE on the GENERAL LABOR TOUR

CHARLIE CHIZONA

ISBN: 979-8-89694-997-8 - Ebook
ISBN: 979-8-89694-998-5 - Paperback
ISBN: 979-8-89694-999-2 - Hardcover

I am dedicating this book to my parents. To my mom, Robbie Sherrill-Howe-Sochacki, and her late husband, Mike Howe, and to my father, Al Sochacki, and his wife, Rustie Sochacki, all of whom showed me unconditional love for over 50 years!

DOWNLOAD THE AUDIOBOOK FOR FREE!

You've got the book, now get the full experience by visiting my website, Chizona.com, where you'll find exclusive content not available elsewhere. To show my appreciation for buying this book, I'm giving you the audiobook for free! Visit the site to claim what's yours—no strings attached, just my appreciation for taking this journey with me.

To claim your free audiobook, visit me here:
https://subscribepage.io/isXeJU

Contents

Introduction

Ay yo. I'm Charlie Chizona, a Chicago guy living in Arizona. I was born in Illinois in 1975. We lived in a ranch-style house in Romeoville.

My parents divorced when I was five. Many people blame their life events on childhood, but I do not. My childhood was a significant part of my life, filled with good times as well as memories and mistakes while I learned from it all.

I lived with my mom, Robbie, and my siblings, Fred and Teresa, in a small suburban neighborhood with parties, cookouts, swimming pools, bike riding (and jumping ramps), wiffle-ball, "war," fort-building, sleepovers, nighttime tag, and every 4th of July, fireworks in the street. You knew your neighbors.

By the time I was twelve, people had moved, neighborhoods had split up, and more privacy fences were dividing secluded neighbors in TV-led households. In 1987, to straighten up my act, I moved in with my father, Al, who had remarried and was living in Warrenville, Illinois, with my stepmom, Rustie, and her two sons, Adam and Greg, whom I consider my brothers. My dad and stepmom later had a daughter, Janice, for whom I babysat when I would have otherwise been getting into trouble. Eventually, I started using my spare time to work and play drums as well.

My spending money would have to come from employment. That was it. I babysat on weekends and did yard work around the neighborhood, pulling weeds and cutting grass. When I turned fifteen, I could obtain a work permit and find a legitimate job.

I had no interest in attending classes of any form. High school required 21 credits to graduate. Most kids finished with an average of 25. I graduated with 21.5. During my entire senior year, I had only one textbook. My days included gym, study hall, art classes, and a period as a teacher's aide to a gym teacher without a class. I used my locker to store food and a jacket. Once eighteen years old, I'd have to pay rent at $35 a week unless I was in college full-time. College? Yeah, right. I couldn't wait to get out of school!

From what I can tell from other people's accounts, college would have been a great party, but for me, the classrooms were a no-go. So, work became a big part of my life at a young age. The general labor section of my local classifieds became my weekly read, even if I was employed. For the longest time I figured I'd be happy with a job where I could simply wear blue jeans. If the jeans aren't faded, torn, or ripped, you can still wear them to certain jobs. For me, blue jeans meant simplicity. Besides, all I had were blue jeans, and I didn't want to go buy work pants.

A Chizona Resume tours four major cities filled with general labor roles I've assumed on the diverse stages of the American workplace, while playing drums on actual stages with local bands. I think of each as a character assigned to recite lines as one who "cares 110%," which I haven't always. As I've played these parts, one leading thing I learned was that *jokesters don't get promoted.* Especially when fun is made at the boss's expense. In my defense, lampooning the boss has been, at times, a highlight of having to work. That, and many bosses make it so easy.

Little did I know my choices would lead me deeper into a lifetime search for the right job, as well as into a greater understanding of my own Rorschach inkblot cards if they were to exist. And so this story begins. Let's have a few laughs, shall we?

Chapter 1

Mom's Early Learning Center

Warrenville, Illinois, 1989

- Maintenance/custodial work/snack delivery
- Total income unknown

There was a short interview to pass for this word-of-mouth position. The manager asked about the basics required for odd jobs and general labor: Are you a citizen of the United States? Do you steal? Can you show up on time when scheduled? Can you work with others? Are you physically able to do this job? Do you have a pulse?

The idea is that if you are alive and responsible, you should be competent. I was a teen in the late 80s in suburban America. Expenses were minimal, and the minimum wage was $3.35 per hour. The job was perfect for my age; teenagers are often the only people willing to do this type of work for such little money.

The position was typically filled by 14- and 15-year-olds, and it entailed showing up each day after school. I worked from 3:30 p.m. to 7:00 p.m. M-F. I reported to a woman who would eat ice cream as she served it. First, I would load carts with ice cream, fruit, and many treats created to be afternoon snacks for kids. Then I pushed the carts to each classroom. Snack-cart delivery makes a person quite popular. After snack deliveries, I cleaned bathrooms, swept, mopped, vacuumed, removed trash, and cleaned the kitchen.

One cool thing about Mom's Early Learning Center was that it was about two miles from home, so I rode my bike to work. The best part of the job was working with three attractive older girls who were employed as classroom teachers.

It put money in my pocket and initiated a lifelong list of work experiences that molded the job machine I would become. You could say this was an introduction to facility maintenance and my awareness that I liked being able to bike to work and wear blue jeans on the job!

Chapter 2

Steve

Warrenville, Illinois, 1989

- Hardware packager/stolen soda suspect
- Total income unknown

Steve, his wife, and their two children lived next to my family in a subdivision. Steve ran a garage business supplying small hardware pieces to various accounts. He'd had employees before me, but reliability was a common issue. I had to walk next door to apply.

My job would be to place basic-sized nuts and bolts into small plastic baggies and laminate them closed. This simple job offered a meager hourly rate, one that Steve would later complain about having to pay.

I started in the summer, and at first it worked out great. Sure, I was working for the neighbor whose kids I might have picked on, but it was close and easy. We used a scale to fill each order. I turned out inventory faster than Steve or his kids. Best of all for me was that I could listen to whatever music I wanted, and I did. I didn't care about the summer heat, either. I never have, which is a saleable asset in general labor.

After summer, school started back up, and Steve's business changed. Instead of ten parts per bag, his primary account wanted each piece bagged separately. Are you kidding me? This was a tragedy. Steve had no way of meeting demand, so he had to try to find other accounts.

He hired a recruiter to help him with this. The guy didn't get much done other than help drink the family supply of soda. Between him and Steve's kids, they were polishing off a case every other day, which was blamed on me. Steve was quiet, not emotional, and even a little bit nerdy. When the frustrations of losing money bubbled up, he began complaining about all his profits going to pay me. At the same time, I selfishly drank his household stock of carbonated phosphates.

I got the impression it was time to seek other employment. I was figuring out that I could work fast if my task was redundant. All I needed were my tunes and to be left alone. I'd enhanced my organizational skills and taught myself new ones. And oh yeah—I was still wearing blue jeans!

Chapter 3

Christopher's Steakhouse

Warrenville, Illinois, 1990

- Busser/leftover scrap from too much hiring
- Total income: $24.70

Some may debate whether a job lasting a few days is worth listing, but experience from even less than a week can still pay off.

While traveling via bicycle, I applied to a new steakhouse that some friends told me was hosting an open-house hiring event. Such establishments tend to over-hire for these types of jobs, perhaps because they can already start clocking the turnover speed as soon as the ink dries.

After completing the hiring documentation, I received rote minimal training on how to bus tables. I was one of the youngest applicants—others were already out of school!

Training me seemed like a textbook waste of time, considering they never called me to work. The episode did however equip me with the standard employee uniform of black pants, white-collared long-sleeve shirt, and black shoes. Just remember: In the beginning, a career path is measured in feet, not miles.

Chapter 4

Subway

Warrenville, Illinois, 1990

- Sandwich artist
- Total income: $352.08

In 1990, the Subway sandwich franchise made its way to my area. Some may be familiar with its branded décor such as bright-yellow benches attached to the table, bright-white walls, and institution-like fluorescent lighting.

I was a sophomore in high school, and Subway was a quarter of a mile from my home. The restaurant hadn't opened yet, so the windows were still covered, but the help wanted sign prompted a visit. I walked in to an on-the-spot interview and was hired by the polite owner, an older, heavier man.

The owner's son thought he was hot stuff. This kid loved to wear his ultra-cool black Ray-Bans. One day, when he left his prized beam blockers on the counter, I colored the lenses with a black permanent marker. Boy was he pissed. I remember people holding him back because he suspected I had done it and wanted to fight me. I never admitted to it, and no one knew the truth, but in the end, the only conclusion to draw was that I had been the instigator. I did learn a few lessons.

One: Don't mess with the owner's kid. Even though I was never reprimanded for the sunglasses incident, everyone figured it was me, which made for a lingering guilty conscience. A prank like that is funny in the movies, but people don't laugh at such things in real life. They call you "rude" or "mean."

Two: Get good at running a cash register. It will set you apart, especially if the employer hires extra staff for a season and needs employees to deal with many customers. Register proficiency communicates skill with counting money and properly distributing change. Customers who are rude to staff have a strange way of changing their attitude when it comes time to pay.

Three: Observe and practice sanitation. At many food-serving businesses, it's a joke. Subway restaurants followed standards that surely helped their rise to success. A job like this gives insight into proper kitchen prep. Foodservice can be seen as a simple job, but it's more complicated than people might think. Maintaining a sanitary workplace is a skill that can be learned. It's one I developed, and I still carry it with me.

Although I can't recall why I left Subway, it left an impression on me. Maybe it was because it was staffed with students from school or was so raw in its ambitious origin. Regardless, it went on to become one of America's top fast-food restaurants. Being among the first to offer self-serve soft-drink machines certainly helped as well. My leftover black pants from my last position came in handy.

My position as a sandwich artist was another that wove facility maintenance into the job duties. I was starting to recognize it as standard.

Chapter 5

Arnie's Pizza

Warrenville, Illinois, 1991

- Kitchen help/facility agitator
- Total income: $1,526.60

Arnold Luczak was a Polish businessperson and a decent guy who owned Arnie's Pizza, a well-known pizzeria in Warrenville. Competition was minimal. In the Chicagoland region, many pizza joints are owned independently, giving the pizza its worldwide renown. What non-Chicagoans should know is that the independent pizzerias we grew up with really were distinctive with great-tasting pizzas.

Arnie's was one of them. Everyone in town ordered from there. Located at the end of a little strip mall, it was known for its white Chevy Chevette delivery car bearing the Arnie's Pizza sign on the top. According to classmates and friends, Arnie's Pizza was rumored to be a "cool" job. One of the various delinquents he had recently employed suggested I apply.

I answered straightforward questions during the interview in the dining room with the kitchen manager. I was able to bike to Arnie's. It was perfect part-time work for a high-schooler. They scheduled me only for a night or two during the week and then Friday or Saturday night.

I was excited to work at such a great pizza kitchen. When you join one such as Arnie's, you quickly find friends asking if they can get free food. That's always a *no*. You don't succeed at a new job by giving away the product. It's the same as stealing.

Many new employees at Arnie's started at the dough machine. It was like a set of stacked laundry rollers, which you ran the dough balls through to flatten them and make the base. The task was to combine giant vats of flour, yeast, water, etc., to make a big blob of softball-sized dough balls and put them on refrigeration trays.

Making the pizza sauce was another new person's job. The procedure involved stirring and mixing the sauce by dipping half of the arm into a plastic bucket full of Arnie's secret recipe, which included sugar for extra pizzazz. I remember my arm stinging from the acid in the sauce. When I think about it now, I would not want people serving me food they'd dipped their arms in. Don't get me wrong—I'm the clean type, and I was back then. But as for others? Can't always trust it.

New-guy tasks included mopping, sweeping, doing dishes, vacuuming and cleaning the dining room, cleaning bathrooms (always a marker of a crappy job, not because of the pun, but because you're thick as thieves with a toilet), and any other grunt work a pizzeria owner might want done. In this case, that might mean cleaning Arnie's car as well.

Answering phones was next, and if you were lucky, you might then get promoted to slicer. The slicer watched for the pizza to finish baking, removed the pie from the oven with a giant spatula, sliced it in seconds with a shogun-like single blade, and boxed it just as fast. I've been slicing pizzas with a large kitchen knife ever since.

I started experimenting with different pies. We sold Italian beef sandwiches, which I especially loved, so I tried putting sliced Italian beef on my creation. I still do it today. I never would have glazed my pizza with barbecue sauce had I not tested it first at Arnie's.

Eventually, Arnie had to replace my spot at the dough machine. Sometimes we took turns tossing tinier dough balls at Arnie when his back was to us. The trick was to make the ball small enough to be less visible but large enough to fling. He only felt it and got pissed off just a couple of times. When he spun around, we didn't look at him and stayed focused on our work. It was easy for me to get away with because I was always on the phone while Arnie prepped pizzas, so I could nail him while speaking with a customer and then keep a straight face, which is an art form. I mean, the dude just got pelted with a dough ball and I had to act like I was clueless! Only two workers were in the room, so it had to be one of us, and Arnie would never interrupt a customer call.

Shenanigans aside, things were going great. I had the job down. Then one day, while I was on the phone, like an idiot I slipped a derogatory note about Arnie on a claim-check form during a stupid exchange with a coworker. Arnie hated using claim checks for anything other than food orders and was known to fish them from the trash. Sure enough, even though my crumbled-up claim check with my unflattering note had been scrapped hours before, he spotted it, took it out, and read what I'd written.

The next time I came in, one employee shook his head while the current manager "had a talk" with me. I called Arnie on his car phone and apologized, but he wouldn't have it. I was fired.

Some of my interpersonal dynamics might have had some distance to go, but I was further developing my skills and experience.

At Arnie's, I learned to be responsible enough to be trusted with opening and closing a facility. I practiced running a register, dealing with phones, and processing orders. I learned inventory management, facility maintenance, and, most important, not to leave a jab at your boss where it can be found.

I picked up excellent pizza tips I kept for life. And, of course, I got to wear blue jeans!

Chapter 6

Dunkin' Donuts

Naperville, Illinois, 1992

- Donut grabber/garden-variety douche
- Total income: $20.00

I responded to a help wanted sign in the window, filled out an application, passed a brief interview, and wore the uniform—including the shirt and (oh God) the hat. It was the summer of 1992, and jobs were not easy to find, especially for a punk like me. But I had a blue 1978 Chevy Monte Carlo, "Blue Thunder," and it needed gas.

I started the Sunday that followed my very brief walk-in interview. When I arrived, the one Asian woman running things set me up at the drive-thru, which seemed like a constant stream of young girls seeking coffee on the go. Naperville was and still is a prominent Chicago west suburb. My friends would commonly refer to its young female population as "Naperville chicks," which typically meant having good looks and a well-off family. And there I was in full uniform, serving donuts and coffee as they rolled past the window. It was embarrassing for me then, but in hindsight, it was a part-time job that put a teenager to work, while adding some money in my pocket, and that is a good thing.

After a few hours of trying to understand my coworker's foreign accent, I left for a lunch break to let the dog out. When I got home, my brother Greg was already there and had done the task, so we sat there and celebrated my extra-long lunch by joking about whether I'd last the rest of the day at Dunkin' Donuts.

As I was returning to work, I remember laughing to myself and thinking, "Am I going back to work at this ratty place?" Upon arrival, I remember the same coworker trying desperately to get me to clean. After about forty-five minutes and a few more Naperville chicks passing by with a glimpse of my hat, I decided, "F this."

I told the woman I had to go out to my car. I took off the ridiculous uniform, got in my car, and split with some Van Halen cranked on my stereo. When I got back home, Greg started laughing. He knew what was up right away.

Although I quit after working four whole hours, I was convinced I deserved compensation. I don't think the owner shared my perspective, because when I went there a few days later expecting money, he told me, "Nah, dude." He didn't use those exact words, but you get the point.

Insisting I deserved four hours of pay, I refused to leave. The owner had already continued serving customers, but he didn't know who he was messing with.

The counter was divided by one of those swinging doors with a bracket to keep it from swinging outward. I proceeded to open and close the half-sized door slightly, making a loud knocking sound that prompted him to tell me to "STOP THAT!" After two minutes of consistent knocking, confused customers, and a determined 17-year-old, he opened the register and grabbed a $20 bill. Satisfied with this gesture, I left with enough to put gas in my tank and buy a case of beer, which I then later brought to a party.

I can still smell the donuts. I guess that's what I learned from that job: Some scents are ruined by working around them. I did realize my workplace socialization needed improvement. What a jerk I was!

Chapter 7

Family Foods

West Chicago, Illinois, 1992
- Stocker/slacker
- Total income: $286.68

A hub for Warrenville, Illinois, residents, Frank's Finer Foods was a large, family-owned grocery store close to our home. I applied there many times and would stop in to follow up because squeaky wheels were supposed to get oiled, but I never received a response.

The store employed many kids in town, including my brother Fred, who, while a junior in high school, moved to my father's house in Warrenville. Fred worked at Frank's for a long time and became the produce manager there. By the time he left, his experience allowed him to land any grocery-store job.

Frank's Finer Foods opened another store just north of us. The second location, Family Foods, held a mass hiring event, where I got hired through a group interview. My job was stocking shelves. I can still remember the grocery-store managers' stress. I kept this evening position until the end of the school year.

The job, which was effortless, taught me standard stocking procedures. Stocking and remerchandising shelves at a grocery store is an endless occupation. However, like many newly opened businesses, they over-hired and could not keep everyone scheduled. The grocery store eventually parted ways with me, as in "You're not fired. We just aren't going to put you on a schedule."

So, there I was, a month into summer without work. The U.S. economy was in a recession and, for teenagers, finding summer jobs was challenging. The black pants and shoes required for the grocery store did come in handy, however.

Chapter 8

Denise Cinquegrani-Kanne

Naperville, Illinois, 1992

- Home and yard renovation/Superman worthy of a sledge-hammer
- $10.00/hour; total income unknown

I was spending a lot of time at my friend Sam Cinquegrani's house. We first met in middle school, and he became one of my best friends, lifelong friends (LLF).

Considering what I've shared thus far, I am pleased to include this position because all I did to get hired was be a friendly, respectful, and reliable associate of Sam.

Denise Cinquegrani, "Mrs. C," was one of those moms whom all your friends love like their own mother: a true angel who always treated others as they should be treated. Mrs. C began celebrating Christmas in the first week of December and spread holiday cheer throughout the month. Mrs. C did a lot for her church and helped struggling families. Mrs. C's sister married a man who owned quarries and a trucking company, Hammerline Trucking. The quarries had houses for employees on the property, usually on a large plot of land that needed constant landscaping. Sam's family lived in those houses throughout the years. My friends and I spent many nights hanging out at Sam's, the "go-to" house.

When Sam's family had to move from the house on the Warrenville quarry to another quarry house in Naperville, we learned the Warrenville house was scheduled for demolition! And so, we waited.

I'll never forget the day before the demolition. Sam picked me up in his silver Ford Ranger, the most rigid pick-up truck ever (I eventually bought a Ford Ranger as well). On demolition day, we found sledgehammers and then just went carnival wild with them. Sam and I enjoyed "breaking stuff," as we had seen David Letterman do to great comic effect on his late-night talk show. Old TVs, furniture, and, of course, drywall—if it was there, it was getting the hammer. The power to the house had been cut, which may have helped reduce risk, but it was an old home, so we did still have to be careful. It was fun.

What I love most about this memory is Sam telling me his grandfather went to remove (and keep) all the light switches and wall sockets, not knowing we'd had a demolition session. Sam's impression of his grandfather throwing his arms up in frustration was hilarious. Sam's grandfather was a man who liked collecting stuff and using tools. He was pretty pissed to find out we trashed anything and everything, but in our defense, those things did smash well.

The Naperville quarry house they were moving into had not been lived in for a while. Over time, things had been "stored" there, meaning the next residents would need to do a lot of clearing out, in addition to weed-pulling, painting, moving furniture, assembling, and whatever else was required to make an otherwise abandoned home ready for occupation.

The quarry homes were distinctive places to live. Mrs. C would pay me and know that if I was at the house by myself for eight hours, she'd return to work that she deemed satisfactory. Her middle son, Chris, might not have considered my painting skills satisfactory, however. He was a blue-collar guy who could have done a better job painting, but as many of us find out with time, plenty of people don't expect utter perfection from our work. If we do our best with an honest effort, it will show.

Mrs. C was sold on my services at the new house starting day one. I cleared out the entire basement of old dry-rotted wood, cobwebs, broken glass, and discarded materials used at quarries. I piled it all up neatly for trash pickup at the end of the driveway. Mrs. C referred to completing that task as "becoming Superman." I'm not the best handyperson, and I certainly wasn't a pro at seventeen. Still, my work ethic paid off. I could pay my car insurance and keep myself productively busy during the summer. It was mainly manual labor, and it continued periodically during the school year.

Working for Mrs. C reinforced for me that self-management is one of an employee's most valuable assets. I developed organizational skills for assessing and navigating workloads, properly disposing of waste, and clearing space through efficient facility maintenance.

Looking back on it now, I include my work for Mrs. C to remind others that we should be professional, respectful, and trustworthy with our work even if it is for friends we're very comfortable with. I treated Mrs. C as we should treat any employer who trusts us with keys to their home to do a job, regardless of what it might be. When we honor the working relationship, we respect the friendship as well.

And oh yeah—Mrs. C let me wear blue jeans!

Chapter 9

Early Times Chimney Sweeps

Lombard, Illinois, 1992
- Telemarketing PITA
- Total income: $71.04

"Wow, telemarketer?"

I'll never forget my grandmother's reaction when I told her about this job. I didn't realize at first that I was one of "those people" calling others at the most inconvenient times. Let's admit it: No moment is good for a telemarketing call.

The Early Times Chimney Sweeps office was in a strip mall in Lombard. The manager was a friendly, heavy-set guy unprepared to manage many high schoolers cold-calling people at dinner time to sell chimney-sweeping services. Word of mouth prompted me to apply, which was followed by an interview that consisted of me showing up and being handed a phone. I had no idea what to expect for compensation. I was just doing something that other kids I knew were doing: calling numbers in the phone book. I remember thinking, "How do we know these people even have a chimney?" Sure enough, on the first night, I was calling people who live in apartments!

The job taught me just how lame telemarketing is, and fortunately, it consumed only a couple of weeks of my life. It reinforced for me telemarketing's status as a widely perceived public nuisance. People were not happy to hear I was doing it, but I could still count on Mom for support (although she hated telemarketers too).

I learned that telemarketers are not allowed to hang up on you. Too bad for them that I now knew that. After I quit, I made it my mission to get telemarketers to hang up on *me*. Anything was fair game to make them consider bothering someone else or finding a different job. Since then, I have been known to test my comedic routine on those who would think to call me with a sales proposition I didn't invite.

I was working with friends and having fun for a minute, but I wouldn't do Telemarketing again—even though it let me wear blue jeans.

Chapter 10

Portillo's Hot Dogs

Naperville, Illinois, 1992
- Hot-dog slinger
- Total income: $63.00

In 1992, Naperville was commercially flourishing with retail stores and eateries. I thought finding another job wouldn't be too difficult even though the country was still in a "recession." I quote that because all it takes, apparently, is some government spokesperson to proclaim in their best Nixon voice, "We are in a recession." People were starting a lot of sentences with "well, in today's economy," and boom, the self-fulfilling cycle continued. Finding a job sucked.

I applied in person as their window advertised and was hired at Portillo's in Naperville. All I needed was black pants, black shoes, and a pulse. So, after a paper application and a quick interview, I began another kitchen job. At first they wanted me to operate a fryer. I'd never had a problem with my face breaking out, and I wasn't about to start, so I quickly helped establish that assignment was out. Another kitchen task was wrapping food and dispensing beverages, which was easy.

I knew I'd be a natural at calling out orders on the mic. This was a disc-jockey job if you made it so. I could do that. I started this role on a Friday-night shift. That first night, I was released to leave without performing closing duties. I had yet to learn what I was "missing" during that time.

When I returned the following day for my Saturday-night closing shift, I worked the same scramble in the super-busy weekend kitchen. I stayed after we closed, and I got a real look at what cleaning the kitchen of a popular restaurant such as Portillo's entailed. Hell no! It was too much, and that was that for me. I made no friendships nor met any females. I felt like a geek wearing that hat and apron. Then again, I was still just a teenager with more to learn and understand. Besides, I liked Portillo's food and still do. If I'd stuck around longer, I would have hated to develop a dislike for the food, especially the jumbo chili cheese dog with raw onions.

I figured there were many other places to look for work right off the bat. Had I known finding another job would be as tough as it was, I might not have been so quick to duck out from Portillo's after only two shifts. I had car insurance and gas to pay for. I applied to all sorts of stores and service businesses. No one was hiring.

Chapter 11

Sizzler of Fox Valley

Aurora, Illinois, 1992–93

- Dishwasher/gringo que no habla español bien
- Total income: $889.44

It was still mid-recession, and hiring freezes existed. By this point, I was searching the general labor sections in the paper for any job. I saw an ad for a dishwasher at Sizzler of Fox Valley that said to apply within. I did so and was called for an interview.

The interview was straightforward. I answered all of the basic questions about reliability. I had no server experience, so they wouldn't put me on the dining floor—I didn't want that anyway. I preferred a standard hourly rate, kitchen schedule, and zero customer interaction. I had transportation, was willing to work weekends, and owned the requisite industry-standard head to toe black clothing required.

Dishwashing is an easy job because it's never complete. Dishes just keep coming. If a job can never be completed, there's no pressure to get it done. Don't get me wrong: I stayed busy. There was plenty to clean, but the industrial dishwashing and sanitizing machines made it simple. A high-powered sprayer hanging from the ceiling was my best friend.

My dishwasher coworkers were all Mexican guys, and they were surprised to see a gringo on the team. They were helpful and friendly and always willing to show me how to do the job right. I used to make up Spanish words as they spoke to one another.

Speaking Spanish is something every American could benefit from. It's not a question of "why do they not speak English?" Rather, learning a second language is self-improvement that can serve us both at work and in life.

Most of my Sizzler coworkers were from the Aurora area. Cute girls were working there too. I tried to go out with a couple of them, but most of them were into techno music and an urban (i.e., hip-hop) look, which placed me out of the bubble. I had a retired police car and a mullet, and I listened to heavy metal.

I worked evenings, so that meant closing, which involved picking up numerous large floor mats, sweeping, and mopping. We sprayed down the incredibly heavy mats. The amount of water used in this operation was unbelievable. Non-slip shoes are vital for this job. There was no slacking. My Mexican coworkers busted their tails and showed up for work daily.

Like any fast-paced manual labor position, I looked forward to breaks. I had a radio near the sink to listen to music, and if I didn't get backed up, I worked alone.

Most of the kitchen guys were glad to have someone reliable handle the sprayer position because they liked bussing tables, which earned tips. I preferred to stay at the sink, spraying food particles off dishes, and loading up the washer and sanitizer. I always stacked cups with cups, plates with plates, etc., which made it easier to put dishes away. Organizing makes a massive difference.

When we work with organized focus and diligence, people take notice. You will outperform many if you follow basic protocols without questioning every step. Combining that quality with reliability will show the manager that you are dependable. When you finally have all the procedures down, you can apply those processes to future jobs.

The starting pay at this job was minimum wage, and after six months, I began to look elsewhere. I wanted to be closer to home because the south end of Fox Valley was at least a twenty-minute drive. When you make minimum wage, gas mileage on an eight-cylinder engine is a significant consideration.

My friends joked about my Sizzler job, but we made fun of one another about everything. I had money coming in, and there was no shame in work that was well-suited for this seventeen-year-old. Summer was coming, and I was graduating. I could soon take a full-time job.

Chapter 12

Angie's Hot Dogs

Warrenville, Illinois, 1993
- Hot-dog slinger
- Total income: $152.98

Yes, another hot dog joint. Anyone who lived in the Chicago west suburbs and traveled Route 59 in the early 90s passed by Angie's Hot Dogs.

They served genuine Vienna-style hot dogs made in Chicago. I always remember Angie's because it was there I first saw a giant glass container full of huge pickles.

I walked in to inquire if they were hiring, and the manager gave me an interview, which consisted of training. I learned that, for certain jobs, apply ready to work.

It was an easy after-school job. The position required minimal skills, such as washing dishes, mopping, and cleaning. Friends were always asking if I would feed them for free, which frustrated me. It's not like employers put you on a register to start giving away their product.

My experience at Angie's was another case of "just be reliable." As long as you keep doing your job, you stay employed. The job kept me from having to change out of my blue jeans and still added experience with facility maintenance, but I needed way more hours.

Chapter 13

Exploring Flooring

Warrenville, Illinois, 1993-94

- Warehouse guy
- Total income: $5,461.00

I graduated high school in June 1993. Afterward, I got my first full-time job by responding to a general labor ad for a warehouse position. Exploring Flooring was in the same strip mall as my former employer, Arnie's Pizza (Chapter 5). The warehouse position was for a permanent, full-time employee, which seemed a good fit for me.

Exploring Flooring was a small outfit run by the owner and his sons. I was interviewed and hired by the administrative assistant. It was a smooth, simple interview due to short answers by me. A nice perk for me was that she had a large Golden Retriever, Buster, who usually took a liking to the warehouse guy and would hang out in the warehouse with me after my hire. I loved it. He had such a big head and always rode shotgun when he was in a car. Seeing his head and eager face in the passenger seat always made me smile.

I spent my first week in the warehouse shadowing the part-time employee who had to return to school. I was surprised by the volume of work and responsibility assigned to us youngsters. We were responsible for all incoming deliveries. This involved operating a pole lift to load twelve-foot rolls of carpet. A pole lift is like a forklift except it has a nine-foot steel pole instead of forks mounted on the front.

Driving the lift was tricky—you had to be mindful. The warehouse was small, with steel support beams throughout. The beams would get the occasional *boing!* from the lift, causing someone to run in and check if I was ok. The lift could cause significant damage to the walls; several holes in the drywall had preceded my employment. To unload the trucks, you had to always reverse down a ramp at a specific angle or you would bottom out and get stuck, or even topple.

Assisting installers was part of the job. I would gather their materials and set them out for an easy start to their day. I would cut carpet for customers and load it into their cars. In the showroom, a lot of expensive rugs for sale were hanging. When customers wanted to see samples of them, I'd bring them down and then hang them back up. Fortunately, I didn't have to work on weekends, but Monday morning, the immediate task was typically organizing after a busy weekend of tossed-around tile and carpet samples.

This position included traditional janitorial duties, such as emptying trash, vacuuming, mopping, dusting, and cleaning windows. After emptying many trash cans, I have to say I developed an aversion to beverages thrown away in the garbage, especially coffee. I cleaned many a trail of drippings back to its origin.

I could climb up on the stacked rolls of carpet, hide, and nap. Occasionally, I had to reorganize the mess an installer or salesperson had made, so I usually planned my roll-organizing when I could cop a few z's.

The owner generously provided lunch every day. He would order take-out from all over town rather than have his staff fend for themselves, and I was always sent to pick it up. I kept inventory in addition to making deliveries and running errands.

The tile room was in disarray before I was hired. From my first day, finding anything, unloading it, and organizing it was a tall challenge. One day with pleasant weather, I decided to tackle the tile room once and for all. I emptied the room and put everything back. From this I learned that the first step in overhauling any storage area is to empty it!

The overhaul was a day-long project. Once the room was clear, I reassembled loose steel-shelving units and assembled unused ones. I created a border along the room's walls using the shelves and made aisles with boxes of tiles to organize and easily count inventory, load, and unload.

My last step of reorganization was stacking grout. I don't know what I was thinking, but I kept stacking and stacking until I heard snapping sounds. The shelving unit I had packed with grout was tipping over—onto me! I tried to stop it by positioning myself and holding my hands up to steady the shelves, but I knew I couldn't support them all, and if they came down on me, I would be a peel-from-the-floor cartoon character. I continued to hold and yelled for help, but no one else was around. With my options highly restricted, I leaped away like a Hollywood stuntman, knocking over stacked boxes of tile as the steel shelving unit loaded with grout crashed down, obliterating the tile it fell on and filling the room with grout powder. As I opened the door, a massive cloud of grout poured out. I was covered in it too. It took two days for me to clean up that mess.

Overall, Exploring Flooring were fair people, and when my shelving-unit incident destroyed tile and grout, their only concern was that I wasn't hurt. In hindsight, I liked that once I had the job down, I could self-manage. I received an education in professional flooring, and it was good to be out of school and working full-time.

Storing and tracking all that inventory gave me insight into properly storing such materials. Operating a pole lift was another skill I developed. Maintaining a warehouse is facility maintenance at its finest. That warehouse could get out of hand quickly, and I learned to make it my own. When you do that, you can run a tight ship and increase your value to the employer. I appreciated the relaxed environment of a blue jean–wearing staff, but the position was a dead-end. I had no interest in carpet installation or sales. After a year I pursued full-time work elsewhere.

Chapter 14

CARQUEST

Warrenville, Illinois, 1994

- Delivery driver/auto-parts smart aleck
- Total income: $2,657.00

I saw a new store opening nearby by the franchised auto-parts store CARQUEST. I applied within and received a simple interview within days. I aced it.

I drove a company pickup truck delivering auto parts. There were computers for checking orders in and out for delivery. There were a few other drivers, mostly smokers who's distinctive perfume of cigarettes greeted me even before I climbed into any truck they drove. On the bright side, smokers weren't permitted to use the newer truck and since I didn't smoke, I could!

I enjoyed driving around and being out and about. I did the work to the best of my ability and learned about car parts. I discovered that a transmission entails more than "just fixing." I came to know just how unfriendly the mark-up on auto parts is to the consumer.

Still being young and restless, just as I had before, I felt the need to move on at a certain point. The manager was a grouch. In this case, I thought it might be better if I were to be let go than to quit. Our company uniform included a stuffy red shirt and a big puffy hat. On one rainy day, I came to work with my own hat on. The manager bolted to the storage area, rumbled through boxes, and came back with the plastic truck driver–style hat with "CARQUEST" on the front. He shoved it into my hands and said, "This is the hat you wear."

I stated I wasn't going to wear it. As I thought he might, he said, "Then walk out that door and don't return until you wear it." I said OK and I left. He was not expecting that, and I did not return. Rather, I gave myself some time off before looking for my next job.

My status as a young journeyman aside, I could wear blue jeans, even though I wouldn't recommend it. Auto-parts delivery tended to be rough on the jeans. If you ever find yourself in a similar role, good old-fashioned navy-blue mechanics pants should serve you well. They leave ample room for air flow when it's hot out, and they're still comfortable enough if you throw on thermals when it's cold. The navy blue does a fine job hiding car-part debris.

Chapter 15

Hammerline Trucking

Lombard, Illinois, 1994

- Snow extractor/salt distribution engineer/company clown
- Total income unknown

My LLF Sam Cinquegrani's uncle owned Hammerline Trucking, which provided snow-removal services. That winter, Sam got us some work. There was no interview; the only requirement was to show up.

Knowing Sam's family, I intended to be respectful and show up on time, but messing around on a job like this was a given. I was with friends. We slacked off, drank hot chocolate, and shoveled snow. Illinois winter winds can find any sliver of exposed skin. I was amazed when others showed up unprepared for the work. I went with the adage that "there's no such thing as bad weather, only the wrong clothes." Shoveling snow can be child's play if you're bundled up properly.

Jobs like this usually have a "pro/old-schooler" on staff, typically the crew leader. These guys can be memorable, and the one on this crew was no exception. Our old-schooler oversaw the shovelers while barely dressed for winter himself. He chain-smoked all day. He had a white mustache and beard stamped with a brown-yellow nicotine stain surrounding his lips. The entire toe section of his right shoe was cut out and exposed to the cold. The toe was swollen, but he didn't seem to care. He referred to anything faulty or broken as "Grateful Dead." For instance, when I went to grab a broken shovel, he said, "Nah, don't use that Grateful Dead shovel."

It was a short but fun and memorable time, especially watching underdressed coworkers ride in the back of snowy trucks from a warm car as I followed. The job would have let me wear blue jeans if I'd wanted to—with thermal underwear, but I wouldn't recommend it. Shoveling snow gets your pants wet, and jeans take longer to dry while freezing your legs in the meantime. Bypass the experiment and just wear snow pants. While the extra cash was nice, I suspect they didn't bring us back for the next storm because of our horsing around.

Chapter 16

Family Ford

West Chicago, Illinois, 1994

- Porter schmuck
- Total income: $3,054.85

Family Ford of West Chicago was advertising a general labor position for an evening porter to work 25–35 hours per week. Pull-time is what I call a job that is neither full-time nor wholly part-time. It sounds better than fart-time. Jobs were hard to get, so "pull-time" would have to do.

Driving a manual transmission was a job requirement many seekers didn't have. I did. I applied in person and was hired a few days later. During the interview, the boss wanted to ensure I knew what the job entailed, but he mostly wanted to determine whether I was dependable and intelligent. I remember feeling like I could be myself in addition to wondering why he had such a big desk.

I worked weekday evenings and daytime on Saturdays. Evening hours were great, as I've always liked to sleep late. I was still living at home, so I had time to help around the house and meet friends after work. Saturdays meant a lot more customer interaction. Family Ford provided breakfast and lunch on Saturdays, which was a nice benefit.

As a porter, you're a lower rung on the ladder. Being down there, I was responsible for basic facility maintenance. I swapped out more license plates than I could count. Today, you get a lot more service when buying a new car, but back then car detailing was something a teenager could do. We had a separate bay just for washing cars. I could park my own car there and keep it maintained. I appreciated parking inside a heated garage during cold, wet, and snowy weather.

All cars had to be accounted for with their keys available. Any time a car was shown, the porter both pulled it up front and drove it back to the lot. Salespeople often requested a quick wash for a potential sale. There was rarely downtime. Even if there were no cars to prep and the bay was running smoothly, the boss wanted me in the lot, cleaning every vehicle.

As the night guy, I had an entire vehicle service department to myself—no other porters, mechanics, or service writers. I listened to whatever music I wanted and took meal breaks when I felt like it. Unfortunately, because the garage was in the back, it doubled as the employee smoking lounge, which drove me crazy. Selling cars must be stressful because almost every car salesperson I ever worked with was a smoker.

This job seated me on what would become my favorite type of motorcycle, the Yamaha Virago. It was a 1983 model with only 500cc, but it was beautiful and in great shape. It had a black-teardrop gas tank, matching panels, and mag-style wheels. A salesperson pushed it into the garage for a cleanup after it had been traded in, and I fell in love at first sight. Family Ford sold it to me for $800 after giving the customer $500. They let me make payments on it, but I had to leave it in the maintenance garage until I paid it off. That baby ran great for a long time until I sold it, regrettably.

This would mark the end of my second summer out of high school, and an opportunity to move into my first apartment had arisen as well. My older brother Greg and I moved into a two-bedroom unit in Glendale Heights close to Route 64 (North Avenue), which was riddled with car dealerships. Finding a job closer to my new home that paid more would be a practical next goal.

Family Ford taught me essential car care and inspired me to start maintaining my vehicle, a valuable life skill. I added another lesson in facility maintenance involving different types of shops and tools to support. I sampled many cars including the Ford Ranger, which I have always liked. My experience driving cars there further informed me of specific criteria to look for when purchasing cars in the future. I was reminded that working weekends could suck, but it was a fantastic job, nevertheless.

I was allowed to wear blue jeans! Sometimes, one's professional and personal dress codes really can meet in the middle.

Chapter 17

Joe Cotton Pontiac

Glendale Heights, Illinois, 1994–95

- Porter schmuck/gopher extraordinaire
- Total income: $11,566.29

Now that I had porter experience, I could seek new opportunities in the same field. I filled out an application at Joe Cotton Pontiac and was called in for an interview by the service manager. During the simple interview, he mostly asked about my experience, references, vicinity, and flexibility.

It was an easy job. However, when a chain-smoker returned from vacation and introduced himself as the porter manager, it was news to me since there was no porter manager position. I only said, "Yeah, okay, man."

After a week, our "porter manager" was making this job seem like it might suck. One of the owners hired a childhood friend, who was a total South Side of Chicago guy, sporting a mustache and slicked-back, balding hair to manage the used-car department. My concerns tapered off as this new used car department manager immediately took a liking to me and assigned me to his department. He was a real wisecracker too. It was great because the used-car department just let me do the job.

The service porter personnel included an ex-con, who worked there briefly. He called everyone "Boss." Although he missed some teeth, he continued to eat chocolate bars while drinking soda. He claimed that part of his prison sentence included pushing a food cart at a women's prison. While doing so, he found that some of the female inmates were grateful when hot dogs were left intact as opposed to cut into slices. That anecdote revealed an aspect of prison life that I hadn't considered.

I liked this job. It was close, and the people were friendly. I ran errands, got lunches, and transported customers and sales staff. I worked indoors in the cooled and heated air. The owners often sent me for ice cream. The mechanics always had good rock stations cranking, and I could get my Ford Mustang LX worked on. I was busy working full-time, which I appreciated

I was having an exhaust problem and terrible acceleration. I worried the repair (or replacement exhaust) would be expensive. A service tech fixed it by replacing a gasket. It took him less than thirty minutes and cost me a whole $20. I vowed never to let car problems go unresolved again. The difference after the repair was huge. The car was quiet with super-smooth acceleration. The dealership later worked a deal with me to trade my Mustang LX for a black Pontiac Fiero that became one of my favorite vehicles to have owned.

My apartment lease was up. I had no plans to quit, but I needed to figure out where I would live. Joe Cotton Pontiac made a change that impacted everything for me overnight.

When I started, there were three owners. One of them suddenly sold his part of the business. Joe Cotton took over and made cutting payroll priority number one. I was first on the chopping block. I went to work and found a missing timecard: never a good sign. I previously dinged a few vehicles. Joe used those dings as the reason for letting me go. The service manager's administrative assistant was tasked with releasing me, which was convenient since her desk was next to the time clock.

From this job I learned that company cutbacks leave nobody safe. I thought porters would be excluded because that job still had to be done. I discovered that many car salespeople double as repo men, and most of them chain-smoke as well. I further realized that being hired for a particular job doesn't always mean it's what you'll do.

If you prove you're reliable and can work without constant oversight, you can get moved to a better position. And, of course, never give them a reason to fire you. Although minor, the vehicle damage came back to haunt me.

Now unemployed with an expiring lease, I moved back in with my parents in Warrenville. On a bright side, I was able to spend the last weeks of my lease off work. Plus, I never had to put on the blue mechanic's uniform, because in the used-car department I could wear blue jeans!

Chapter 18

Oil-X-Change

Warrenville, Illinois, 1995

- Tech/grease monkey/imitation mechanic
- Total income: $400

Tech is the title given to those who raise a vehicle, unscrew a plug, let the oil drain, twist off and replace a filter, lower the car, and add new oil. Tech. OK, we'll call it that.

I was back at my parents' home. I decided to try the local Oil-X-Change because they employed many kids from town. My older brother Fred had worked there briefly.

This job was easy to get. Oil-X-Change never took down the "Now Accepting Applications" sign. The hiring process was standard: Complete the application; wait; call a few days later to show eagerness for the job; appear for an interview and answer simple questions; provide brief, unobjectionable answers; and start ASAP. My experience as a porter came in handy too.

I worked at Oil-X-Change for a week. By now I'm hoping it's apparent that I was trying to work at least one week at a job before deciding it sucks. I didn't always reach that goal, of course, but it was the target.

We worked ten hours or more with a lot of manual labor each day. Cleaning up oil is repetitive activity, considering it will only be done again in less than twelve hours.

It's always good to have vehicle knowledge, and the job taught me about how different vehicles function. It had decent pay, and promotion was possible.

One of my coworkers had a side hustle filling gumball machines. The machines dispensed trail mixes, M&M's, or gumballs for a quarter. On one slow day at the shop, he was spray-painting disassembled machines. After spray-painting the machines, he reassembled them and filled each with the various snacks from large buckets with his bare hands. Mind you, he changed oil for a living and just used spray paint! I'll never lose my slow-motion mental image of his hairy, oil-stained hand and forearm reaching into those buckets, scooping out candy and trail mix, and emptying it into paint-fumed machines. The sight was dreadful. There are no regulations on food dispensed from gumball machines. Life lesson: *Do not ever eat from a coin-operated gumball machine.*

Because I was living with my parents, I didn't need a job so badly that I had to work six long days a week coming home filthy and tired. That would mean not having much left in the young gas tank to enjoy time with friends. One weekend in that motor oil covered mechanics brown uniform was all it took to determine this job wasn't a fit.

Chapter 19

Painter's USA

Wheaton, Illinois, 1995
- Exterior/interior paint application specialist
- Total income: $2,550.00

I saw a general labor ad for full-time painters with the magic words "will train!" The ad said to apply in person. Being unemployed, I had time to walk in dressed properly, nice and early, apply, interview and get hired right then and there.

The hiring manager wanted to know the basics: reliability, availability, and whether I would acquire the necessary items to perform the job (white painter's pants and pro quality painting supplies).

I was put on a crew that included the foreman, who stared at women as if he'd never seen one, and a non-peaceful hippie (or what I call a "hippiecrite")- a total hothead who seemed to want to fight everyone except me and the foreman. We worked outside, which freed him to chain-smoke as well.

I was learning commercial painting. The office sent me on a one-week assignment with "pro/old-schooler" Louis. This guy was impressive! Louis was a retiree who worked for the activity of it. His white Ford Aerostar minivan was a fully stocked traveling paint shop. I could not believe how organized and detailed he was. This is when I learned that no job is too difficult—only the wrong tools make it so!

Louis and I were to work on an old Catholic church with multiple ledges, ceiling corners, balconies, and ceiling fans that needed dusting with a shop vac. Our job included unloading a colossal trailer of heavy-duty scaffolding and setting it up inside the church before vacuuming. Scaffold-building is tedious and tiring, and it must be done right to prevent a collapse. We spent the first day building the scaffolding up to about a story and a half with a base on wheels. We vacuumed as much as possible during the next two days. On the last day, we got to the final section that was up one step. We had a choice: tear down the scaffolding and build it up again on the platform or try to move it up to the one step. Louis decided we should tilt the scaffolding and move it up the step. HUGE MISTAKE!

We tore down about a quarter of the length and tried raising the tower slowly. When we got one side up, it looked promising, and we began to roll it. Then we heard a loud snap. I immediately had flashbacks to the grout-filled shelving unit falling on me, and the entire scaffold started tilting to one side. Louis whisper-yelled, "Oh crap, jump!" So, we did. The second Hollywood stunt leap of my career was followed by the loudest crash I've heard. I don't know how no one else heard it.

When the dust settled, the scaffold was scattered all over the platform and the marble podium where the priest would stand to give sermons was split. We reported the incident at once, and surprisingly, the only concern was our safety.

After that incident, I was assigned back with the foreman and the hippie to paint the outsides of buildings in an apartment complex, which was at least a month's work. The assignment was perfect because the complex was close to my home. I wouldn't have to meet and follow them in the morning, or ride together in one car. I preferred having my car in case I could leave early or had to stay late.

The apartment contract was fun during pleasant weather. We listened to our tunes and worked at our own pace. Anytime I can work alone and listen to my preferred music, I'm happy. I was OK with working late on Fridays, especially if I had the weekends off.

In the end I lost this job because we lacked enough business. The apartment complex had taken us into fall, and all the outdoor jobs were done. So, back to the general labor ads I went. Standard white painter's pants are perfect for this job. I wouldn't dare wear blue jeans on a paint site.

Chapter 20

Careers USA Temp Services

Bottling plant in West Chicago, Illinois, 1995
- Stacker/wrapper/robot
- Total income: $1,314.00

I responded to a local general labor section ad seeking "warehouse help." This could mean different things, all with specific equipment for the items of trade. Working in a warehouse is fascinating because you see brilliant inventions, procedures, and solutions created by people who aren't considered smart. I met many inspired, talented people in the warehouse who were less equipped at managing life.

The warehouse job was advertised through a temporary agency, which was both good and bad. Temp agencies are good because they can put you to work right away; there are many options to choose from and if you don't steal, fight, or otherwise make an ass of yourself, you could get placed elsewhere if the first position isn't working out. The downside to working for a temporary service is a more-vigorous vetting process (i.e., multiple interviews) and you are labeled a "temp" by coworkers unless you become a permanent hire.

I started at a bottling plant that molded small thick, plastic tubes into two-liter soda bottles and ran 24/7. The position required earplugs, steel-toed boots, and the ability to stand for twelve hours. They offered me the graveyard shift from 7 p.m. to 7 a.m. My schedule would alternate: four days on and three days off, and then the following week, three days on and four days off. I loved having four days off in a row. I got three breaks for each twelve-hour shift. A fifteen-minute break can be a big relief when your shift covers half of a day!

The mold machines were huge and loud. My job was to stand behind a yellow safety line painted on the floor, monitor the machines, and retrieve any of the plastic parts that popped out onto the floor (which happened often enough to create a job for it). When the boxes of bottles were filled, I stacked them on a pallet and wrapped them with large rolls of industrial-strength plastic wrap to be picked up by the forklift.

This job was dull, monotonous, and tiring on the feet. It could have been steady long-term employment with benefits, and an opportunity for promotion—if you became a permanent hire. But after a couple of months, it was clear that I would not be brought on permanently, which was OK. I had added to my warehouse skills and renewed my respect for safety procedures.

Plus, I was paid well and I could wear blue jeans. When working warehouse shifts, I was still strongly behind the idea that the simpler and more comfortable the uniform, the better.

Chapter 21

Paramount Parking

Chicago, Illinois, 1994–99

- Valet parker/rock star/smart aleck from hell
- Total income unknown

Paramount Parking was unique because it served as a primary or secondary source of income for years, depending on what was going on in my life. Realistically, to possess as many roles as me, you would need to work multiple jobs at one time.

Lifelong friend (LLF) Dave Bon founded this company in the 1990s, and it was my first job parking cars. I first met Dave in 1989, when I was fourteen and he was roommates with my brother Greg. Dave had moved downtown and started Paramount Parking. Dave successfully ran Paramount Parking with the help of Greg and another brother of ours, Adam, so I joined the team. Valet parking, if done right, can be a blast!

My first shifts were only on Saturday nights because weekday shifts were always filled. But I got to hang out downtown on a Saturday night in the required black pants or shorts. Employee meetings were held at Dave's house, and attendance was mandatory for shift opportunities. It was interesting to see how valets acted one way on the job and another at meetings.

The challenge in Chicago was to have a parking lot. Our Bella Vista account was located at Belmont and the Sheffield Avenues. It was a great spot that really let me learn Chicago. Bella Vista really liked Paramount Parking. I worked that busy account with Adam and Greg.

At first, Paramount Parking just called me in when a shift needed covering, usually on a Saturday. I would enthusiastically drive to Chicago, eat excellent (and typically complimentary) food, and meet diverse people. We had a designated lot for Bella Vista, which was valet gold, and it fit lots of cars. We were all in great shape because we were constantly running. It was fantastic physical conditioning.

In time I got to the point where I would open and close, which meant I could be trusted to work alone. On one of those solo nights, Bella Vista got swamped with diners, and the restaurant owner asked if he could "help" me. A Porsche 911 pulled up, and the restaurant owner said, "I'll take this one. I race Porsches!" And then he *stalled* it! I laughed, and of course, he saw me. Getting laughed at tends to piss people off. Adam showed up to provide actual help. When Adam began explaining how "Charlie was putting cars....," the restaurant owner interrupted him, yelling "F--- Charlie!"

Greg got me a couple shifts where he was managing the valet service at another restaurant in the area, Mia Francesca, which was busy seven nights a week. On slow nights, the wait for dinner was at least twenty minutes. On busy nights, it ran up to ninety! Mia was a fabulous account. Weekday accounts were sought after, and this one provided steady work, spectacular money, and top-notch food. It was even frequented by Michael Jordan, who had his car valet parked.

To provide immediate service, valets stand outside regardless of the weather conditions. As a valet driver, I had to relay the wait times to each customer so they could decide whether to wait. Many valet customers don't recognize that the valet's job is the same whether they stay five minutes or five hours. Some customers believe that leaving the establishment early means the parking service is free. Customers who hand their keys to the valet should understand the same work is involved for any length of stay and expect to pay the fee for it. When you're in the city, you'll rarely have a choice about whether to valet your car.

Mia Francesca did not have a dedicated parking lot. Dave rented a lot for all nearby accounts but it was a far run and used only when we got real busy. We mainly used metered street parking near the restaurant.

Valet parking without a designated lot in Chicago really is rough. The city has sticker parking in most neighborhoods, and it's closely monitored. Chicagoans have likely seen a ticket flapping from under their windshield wiper at some point. With Mia, I learned to get creative. Employees from the account would valet with me, so I used their cars, as well as my own to occupy two spaces. I would place the city issued orange envelope on the window so as to appear as if already ticketed for meter violation.

Working the Mia account was valet boot camp: an all-weather, tactical assignment. Valet parking might seem as if it'd be easy to work in, but many people are not good at it. The job requires the ability to operate a manual transmission, self-manage, work a solo shift, and maintain the entrance.

Eventually, I got a regular shift on Friday and Saturday nights at Blues Etc., one of two well-known blues bars under the same owner. There was one setback, I wasn't yet twenty-one years old and could only enter the bar to retrieve or hang keys in the key box. Bars were smoky; I preferred my outdoor position.

At first I worked on the Blues Etc. account with two other valets. In time I became confident enough to run my own show. In addition to serving customers, I dealt with panhandlers, vagrants, homeless people, and general street wackos. Theft and vandalism of customers' cars and intentionally interfering with business were legitimate concerns. It was excellent experience in people management. Dave rented a small parking lot across the street from Blues Etc. that wasn't available until 11 p.m., so for three hours, we had only street parking to operate with.

Keeping the Blues Etc. shifts filled were challenging for Paramount. The bar wanted the same person for both weekend nights. I had no problem with it because I lived in the burbs and loved going downtown on Friday and Saturday nights. I stayed at Dave's place or my brother Greg's.

Working this account every weekend gave me excellent parking practice. During one of my Saturday shifts, Robert Plant of Led Zeppelin showed up to see the band playing that night. He was dropped off with a security group in a white cargo van with tinted windows, so there was no parking it for me. Few people knew it was him because his hair was fully tucked up into a winter cap, and he was wearing a tie-dyed Jimi Hendrix t-shirt over a white long-sleeved thermal shirt. I exchanged brief greetings with him when he was on his way out. He was tall, and to my surprise, he drank Miller Lite.

That night was so busy I must have run fifty cars, parking most of them on the street. Zero keys were lost (or locked in a car), no vehicles got parking violations, and no damage was done. Dave was so impressed that he let me keep all the money the account made that night.

Blues Etc. was on a street corner with a small but necessary loading zone. You wouldn't believe how many motorists, especially taxis, pulled into the loading zone, claiming they would "only be there a few seconds." The only thing a valet could do was wait it out, and they knew it. I would respond by blocking them in with cars and then run off shouting, "I'll be back in a few seconds!"

There were always late-stayers at the locations where we valeted. I learned that when frustrated by a "lingerer," I could accept the situation and work an angle that favored the gratuity, which often went my way. At Blues Etc., my shift usually ended about thirty minutes after the bar closed. You wouldn't believe how many people left the bar without claiming their vehicle. A lot of them thought I would just wait for them until they came back from wherever after closing. Some left us with no choice but to find the closest street spot in front and leave the keys with the bar. We would leave a note asking them to read the entire valet ticket, which identified the hours of service.

I worked the Blues Etc. account for nearly a year, until I got a Wednesday-night shift at a bar in Bucktown called Mad Bar. I always joked they should have spelled it MADD Bar, with an extra D, to emphasize madness. Wednesday night was ladies' night, and at the time, I was wearing braces, which as you can imagine made me a hot candidate for those in attendance. It was another account we had gotten savvy with regarding street parking, and I ran it alone. It was a simple five-hour shift with excellent tips.

I was still working on this account when I turned twenty-one and my teeth were brace free. I had a lot of Wednesday nights out in the city after work. Even though I closed at 2 a.m., it was still early in Chicago and several bars on the north side were open until 4 a.m. The key was to spend only a little of the money you just made.

Waking up after spending more than you earned the night before isn't enjoyable.

Now a "legal adult," I had no restrictions on parking for bars, making possible the nightclub accounts managed by Adam on Halsted Street. This area was the most lucrative hub for parking and Dave rented a larger lot just north of Fullerton owned by Chernin's Shoe Outlet on Halsted.

No matter where we were scheduled in the city, the Chernin's Shoes lot was our hub after a shift. Adam always had food and drinks. In wintertime, he kept ice-cream bars in the trunk. It may have been below thirty-two degrees, but running for cars kept us warm, and eating ice cream outside in the middle of a Chicago winter didn't faze us.

Having shifts at different accounts allowed me to become a familiar face to all the door and staff members, which meant when I went out, I never waited in line or paid a cover. Drinks were comped or at least discounted.

Many may feel they can identify with valet parking because they have worked in a rapid service atmosphere. Having worked in various service fields, I can identify how valet service differs. Valets must deal with far more people than just direct customers, and in my experience, most complaints came from individuals who weren't valet customers. On one occasion, Dave took a phoned-in complaint from an angry non-customer who didn't realize he was griping about Dave to Dave. It was a decorated story filled with lies, so Dave assured the non-customer that the person in question, Dave the valet, would be fired. Dave fired himself after the phone call and then rehired himself the following morning.

I later got a shift at Soul Kitchen—named after the popular Doors song—which was famous for its Cajun food. They were great to valet for. Like any reasonable account, Soul Kitchen fed the valets every night. With this shift I enjoyed working with my brother Greg. We managed the account seven days a week. In addition, Adam ran the nearby self-park that Greg and I used for Soul Kitchen cars. Because of where the restaurant was, pulling the car up for a customer could be tricky, so we often used the back alleys.

They had long wait times each night. Relaying those times to customers was essential to prevent parking a car only to retrieve it right after because the guest decided not to wait. The Soul Kitchen was one of my favorite accounts and bared much fruit.

There was plenty of nearby nightlife, including several 5 a.m. bars. The Blue Line stop at Damen Avenue was within walking distance as well. We made great money and met tons of people. As valets, we were true "flies on the wall." You would not believe what people did as if we weren't there. They would litter, party, start fights, and even attempt theft!

Soul Kitchen was located next to an 800-person capacity nightclub called the Double Door, where local and touring acts played nightly. Soul Kitchen's exit led right out to our loading zone, which was connected to the club's band loading zone.

One Tuesday night, as I opened the valet shift at Soul Kitchen, the Double Door had a large tour bus occupying most of the two loading zones. The road manager of that evening's headliner approached me and introduced himself as Gooch. He asked me to valet for the band, The Smashing Pumpkins. I agreed, and we guided the bus driver to our lot.

I was asked to keep the sold-out show private, but I told my brothers and Dave. I parked the individual Volvos for three of the band members: James Iha, D'Arcy Wretzky, and Matt Walker (replacing original drummer Jimmy Chamberlin). Lead band member Billy Corgan arrived separately with his family in a minivan. It was a super-busy night going in and out of the club, with crowds hanging out on the street to hear the Pumpkins. It was a memorable reward for a double-duty-hoof-it-all-night. I was still working well after Soul Kitchen had closed for the night. That's city life: Anything can happen any day of the week.

Through this job, I started getting good at serving a wider base of clientele and operating many kinds of vehicles. I finally understood Chicago geographically. It can be confusing, but once you know "the Grid," it's straightforward. Nevertheless, valet parking and being of legal age were fantastic. I wouldn't dare do this job in blue jeans, but it's attitude was ever so present.

I learned a lot about people by parking their vehicles. Many people make assumptions about others according to the car they drive. I can attest that judging another person by their car is not remotely accurate when evaluating who they are as a person. Quite a few customers thought their car deserved more attention and security than everyone else's. Some, even believing that valets joy-ride as if they were having me park a Ferrari. None of them did. Trust me, I'm not interested in joy-riding your BMW.

Regrettably, outside of air-drumming while listening to music on headphones, playing the skins had fallen by the wayside for a while. Being in the city was reigniting my flame, and my fire would spread to Dave, who started playing guitar and singing again (he always had a talent). He and his brother, Ross, who was the lead singer for the popular Chicago band The Mighty Blue Kings, had set up a drum kit in their apartment, and I started to use it for practice.

After observing The Bandoleros every Wednesday night at Mad Bar, I even picked up my salsa beat and applied it to my drumming. Blues Etc. influenced me further as a musician. The blues, drumming, and song foundations were embedded in my subconscious every

Friday and Saturday. For a long time, I had avoided the blues, but eventually you must accept what you grew up with. If you're from Chicago, you gots da blues—and I do.

Chapter 22

Valet Systems

Lombard, Illinois, 1995

- Valet/vehicle-placement engineer
- income unknown

Maggiano's of Oak Brook contracted Valet Systems for their car-parking service, and friends working there got me a lunchtime shift Tuesday through Friday. It was awesome because it never interfered with any Paramount Parking shifts.

Valet Systems had the typical snoozer mandatory training and new-hire orientation in which people "motivate" you with time-consuming boredom and irrelevant isolated-incident stories.

I distinctly remember one manager with whom I'd gone to high school. He was a year older. I didn't recognize him at first because he had lost considerable weight. In his orientation lecture, he highlighted weight loss as a benefit of the job, and it was a good motivator for those who wanted to shed pounds. Exercise is easier when it's your job. I never minded the running that valeting required; I was used to Chicago, where I always had to run distances. Some people even tipped extra generously if they saw your hustle. Valet work is four to eight hours of cardio several times a week. Trust me: It's good for the body.

Working the Maggiano's account was memorable. It was a simple account to run, and we horsed around a lot. Daytime valet parking at a suburban mall was considered "cake." No cabs, buses, pedestrians, vagrants, or cops like down in the city. No weekends! If management started proposing weekends, you fought it with any excuse you could quick-draw: "I work another job on weekends, I have to take care of my parents, I'm babysitting my nephew." Parking was plentiful and you could stack cars like crazy without keystone cops ticketing.

The fee for valet parking at Maggiano's was $4 per car, which meant pulling in $5 bills all day. Valets never worked past 3 p.m. unless they were closing the stand at 5pm.

While the valet parking was for Maggiano's, it was set up in front of The Corner Bakery, a well-known, upscale deli franchise with a larger presence in California, Texas, Pennsylvania, and Illinois. It's where I discovered tiramisu. Their managers hooked us up with food. We never minded parking their cars. This easy shift was fantastic while I lived in the suburbs. It paid daily, offered convenient hours, and was a pleasant change of pace from the chaos of parking cars in Chicago.

However, we were still a bunch of dudes off the chain without accountability. Right before I started, the owner of Valet Systems was in a severe car accident. That left him out of commission and the business without an owner. Money wasn't turned in, and valets ran each Valet Systems account however they wanted. The lack of consistency created a growing web of problems.

We'd been running a tab of faded, ripped blue jeans conduct that forced Maggiano's to report a long receipt of complaints to Valet Systems. Our shenanigans caught up with us, and Valet Systems fired us all.

Chapter 23

Carpetland USA

Lombard, Illinois, 1996

- Warehouse and receiving/guy in the back
- Total income: $978.25

I complied with a general labor ad to apply in person at Carpetland USA for an evening warehouse position. Yes, another warehouse-guy position. For a while, I'd started to consider "warehouse guy" an actual career title.

Another brief interview, another immediate hiring. I worked this extremely easy job 3 p.m. to 8 p.m. Monday through Friday. On Wednesdays I got out just in time to work my valet shift at Mad Bar in the city. I had a sweet valet schedule on Wednesday and Saturday nights while doing this pull-time [see Chapter 16] warehouse day job close to my basement cavern in Woodridge. I could sleep late!

People shopping for rugs can be demanding if they are with an interior designer—ugh! Climbing up a ladder to take down and re-hang large area rugs as customers made buying decisions is not simple work. On the plus side, interior designers might tip for service, send lunch as a gesture, and act as solid references for other employment.

I knew I needed to do the job as they wanted. As I've alluded to, once an employer knows you're competent, you can sometimes then do it your way. The evening parts of my shifts were usually spent cutting up unused carpet from installations into remnants, cutting pads for walk-in customers, and providing carry-outs for customers. Occasionally, deliveries showed up, but trucks were typically off the road by late afternoon. I could listen to my music of choice while I worked.

I got better at running a pole lift and maneuvering the twelve-foot rolls of stacked carpet (this time with notably less drywall damage). It was the same job as at Exploring Flooring, except with a more-extensive facility.

I spent time retagging the rolls with bright-green signs to be visible from afar. *Lesson: If you see a solvable problem, address it.* Creating solutions, even for small stuff, and reducing steps for greater efficiency make us and our workplace more productive while showing we are team players.

I could park at the rear loading dock and on slow days clean my car. I felt fine not locking my car doors in the back until someone went in there and stole my workout bag. I mention this to call out how stupid some people can be. The workout-bag thief didn't bother looking in the center console, where two nights' worth of valet money was wrapped in their daily sheets. There was at least $100 in cash—easy money!

Working alone was still consistently forming into a way of life for me. Some people just operate better independently than among a crowd. At Carpetland USA there were always tasks to perform and tools within the work area I could use. The plentiful carpet samples proved to be a diversely useful life tool as well. Hopefully by now, you've learned that I reuse stuff.

The schedule was perfect, the location was close to home, I wore my blue jeans, and they didn't care about my long hair: all factors I looked for when job hunting back then.

Wintertime came, and I wasn't looking forward to it. I'd just turned twenty-one, and I had family in Phoenix. I decided to start the general labor tour with the first stop that would turn out to be a six-month vacation!

Chapter 24

Frank's Landscaping

Phoenix, Arizona, 1997

- Landscaper/link in a chain gang
- Total income unknown

My mom was remarried to Mike Howe. His son, my stepbrother Mike Jr. and I headed to Phoenix just in time for winter. It was an incredible road trip. Snow and cold temperatures followed us from the Windy City to Winslow, Arizona.

When we finally arrived in Phoenix, Mike Jr. and I worked a landscaping job lasting a few weeks for a family acquaintance named Frank. Shoveling rock and pushing wheelbarrows full of rocks and stones in Arizona was one of the toughest jobs I've ever had. We felt like convicts. It sucked. And it was January! I couldn't imagine doing the work during the Arizona summer.

Frank mainly utilized his three live-in laborers from Mexico, so Mike Jr. and I were included as extra help for a couple of big jobs as needed.

Whenever I have a job that involves physical labor, I often share this experience to offer further perspective to those who think they might be working hard. Beyond baking in the Southwestern fire oven, it paid $8 per hour and started at six a.m. After pushing loaded wheelbarrows all day, you often went home with blisters and sore muscles to show for it. The schedule might range from two hours to zero to twelve.

After a brief time, it became clear Mike Jr. and I shouldn't work together if the goal was getting stuff done; we joked around too much. For example, we'd nicknamed Frank to Stank because he was annoying and his attitude needed a wrench turn, as did his overall demeanor.

I could wear blue jeans on this job, but it meant ruining them with the labor conditions. It was a lesson on the comfort of jeans in the desert driving me to wear shorts, which was less safe. Aside from that education, I learned that landscaping requires a lot of heavy, sweaty exertion. Besides, we were with Stank only for immediate cash flow until we could find something else, and Stank didn't need us that much anyway.

Chapter 25

Apple Moving

Phoenix, Arizona, 1997

- Mover/helper/rat
- Total income unknown

After shoveling rocks, anything was doable. I responded to a general labor ad for a moving company. Moving companies are always hiring. I was about to find out why.

This position was yet another instance of me getting a job simply by filling out the application in person. Apple Moving was a family-run business. I didn't fully appreciate my hiring because being from Chicago and having just moved to town, I was considered a possible snowbird, and snowbirds are high-risk hires in Arizona. So, I was lucky to have the job. Right?

Operating a moving business is simple, and it can be run efficiently by people with basic organizational skills. I'm not big, so when people see me, they don't typically think "carrier of big things." Despite that and my lack of experience, Apple Moving hired me anyway.

I was paired with an older guy who wasn't much bigger than me. He was a smoker—ugh! Like most smokers, he acted on every chance to chain-smoke. He kept those tar-and-nicotine sticks close to his face like a true addict and drank Mountain Dew all day. He did teach me to properly move furniture in a brief time.

We would do multiple homes in ten-hour days, six days a week at first. I discovered that Saturdays will always be necessary for this service. It's interesting how much you can gain from a job if you commit to learning. When you "hump" furniture, you get real-life physics lessons in leverage and momentum. We applied cleverness and ingenuity in place of physical size and brute strength. Our tools included straps, moving blankets, packing tape, plastic wrap, and hand trucks. We wrapped corners and always removed the inside of a hideaway bed. I don't care what the customer says about the history of moving it—always remove the hideaway bed from the couch. That also goes for the legs on a couch. Doing this ensures that you don't damage walls. It makes the sofa more manageable to fit through doorways and stack. Discourage a customer who insists on keeping them on. Sometimes, the legs are in there permanently, which stinks, but you can still bubble-wrap them.

Still another thing I learned was to never make an empty-handed trip. For example, if you have to go to the truck for tools or supplies, take something out with you, even if it's just a lamp or a box. I have used that principle to this day when transporting music equipment, groceries, camping gear, and much more.

While we did meet people who opined we "didn't look like movers," if you have two experienced movers willing to do it correctly, that's all you need. If volunteers are there to "help," no thanks. In my experience, most volunteers who were "helping" had difficulty taking direction. Moving is a perfect example of when explaining what you're doing takes longer than completing the task.

We preferred being able to do our job when the homeowners were not present. With our tools and a ramp to the truck, we could safely move an entire home in half a day on our own.

The probable tips were worth it although some customers can be testy, petty, and intrusive. When customers no longer wanted decent furniture and planned to give it away, I was right there to lay claim. It was amazing how many people packed the truck with "donations."

A moving job brings you into different people's homes daily, making you realize how gross and disgusting some people can be. Regarding personal belongings, it's incredible how "brand new" everything was. Having camera phones back then would have helped with all the claims people made.

A moving job that teaches you about various parts of a new city daily is a positive thing when you are in a new town. From what I've seen, moving attracts heavy smokers. I don't enjoy working with smokers, no matter how great they are as people or how well they do the job. After a month of smoke-assisted labor-intensive work, I kept job searching.

I was still staying with family, which made job hunting less stressful. As much as I loved working in blue jeans, my blue jeans and I had yet to encounter an Arizona summer.

Chapter 26

Big O Tires

Phoenix, Arizona, 1997

- Door-to-door sales annoyer
- Total income: $42.50

This was a perishable door-to-door sales position and a "make your own hours" arrangement.

I honestly have no recollection how I met the two company reps that had me wear a Big O Tires shirt and handed me a handful of coupon cards to sell door-to-door for $100 each. The cards offered twenty discounted services. In the late 90s, the country wasn't yet run by cell phones, emails, and credit card sliders on tablets, so on the rare occasions we sold coupons, we got a check or cash.

Door-to-door sales is a crappy job. You instantly annoy most people. You could offer $20 bills to people and still get doors slammed in your face. Who knows what's opening the door when you knock?

Sometimes, being unemployed can provide an edge in getting hired. The ability to say "I can start tomorrow" is valuable.

As much as I loved wearing blue jeans when I worked, which I could have done with this job, I was finding they didn't suit me as well when walking for a while within the Phoenix heat. My Illinois legs got accustomed to shorts for this very brief occupation.

Chapter 27

Marina del Sol

Phoenix, Arizona, 1997
- Yard guy/porter/boat chump
- Total income: $992.50

Armed with experience in facility maintenance, I responded to a general labor ad for a boat-yard porter by applying in person. The interviewing manager was from Chicago, which gave me an advantage, although he was concerned about the snowbird effect. I still hadn't spent a summer in Arizona. I got the job, as they needed to fill the position after recently firing the last guy.

The city of Phoenix had begun mounting bike racks on the fronts of buses. Given that this boat dealership was far from home, this was how I commuted.

It was decent work. The wash area was in a covered outdoor bay with all the tools I needed and I could jam to my tunes. The first order of daily business was to use a forklift truck to move each boat from the backyard to the front. Each boat was on its trailer with a hitch. The forklift had a trailer ball (instead of forks) that was inserted into the trailer hitch. My experience driving pole lifts at carpet warehouses came in handy.

The store received new boats delivered by transport. I was responsible for unloading, staging, and inspecting them. A good inspection takes time and could suffer with an impatient transport driver. Inspecting is important because any defect must be reported before signing off for each boat. When a new boat was sold and scheduled for delivery, I would clean it. This was a critical part of the job. It's not just spraying water and wiping. The boat had to be completely detailed.

There were two rainy days, and during one of them our Wisconsin native boat mechanic joked, "We get a couple of these a year." That comment stuck with me long after. Strangely enough, I can't remember why I left this excellent blue jean wearing job.

Chapter 28

Interwest Personnel Services

Phoenix, Arizona, 1997

- Trench creation/shop help
- Total income: $585.00

After a few months in Arizona, I moved in with Mike Jr., who was living in south Phoenix. I was now within biking distance from Tempe, which opened some job opportunities.

We responded to a general labor ad by a temporary agency looking for general laborers. We dug trenches on a construction site for $8 per hour on our first assignment. It was an early shift that ended by 3 p.m. Mike Jr.'s having a car was a huge asset. It sat only two, so there was no need to worry about giving rides to anyone else. Working together was fun. We joked around constantly.

One day, the two of us were sent to a steel factory, where they started us with a couple of push brooms and basic cleanup in their storage area. We were laughing it up and making the best of it. Some people can be threatened by those who have fun while they work. We were told, "Instead of wasting time talking, you should be working." Whatever. Properly pushing a broom while conversing was well within my capabilities.

Mike Jr. and I nicknamed the floor manager "Luke Duke" because of his feathered hair. We instantly annoyed Luke Duke. We must have been talented at it too because they fired us halfway through the day refusing to sign our slips, meaning we wouldn't get paid from the temp agency. Mind you, Mike Jr. was short-tempered. Luke Duke tried to intimidate us with a stare-down and told Mike Jr., "Yeah, you got a mouth on you." I had been neutral until that point. The way he said it was so weird! Mike Jr. and I looked at each other and burst out laughing.

Of course, they insisted we leave right then and followed us out fearing we might damage things on our way out. We didn't. They may have dressed in blue jeans, but they were not cool.

Coincidentally, we didn't get any more job offers from the temp agency.

Chapter 29

Roadrunner Staging Inc.

Phoenix, Arizona, 1997
- Totally pumped roadie
- Total income: $176.00

Mike Jr. had been working here and there for a local company called Roadrunner Staging. After the short-lived temp-agency episode, we got a call from Roadrunner Staging saying they had acquired two big contracts for major concerts coming to town and quickly needed to hire a couple of dozen people. With gigs like this, you can usually get an "in" with the company after working a few times.

This call came with additional fantastic news. My family and friends know the Canadian rock band Rush is my all-time favorite. I had known they were coming to Phoenix, but I hadn't gotten tickets yet because of a lack of funds. When Mike Jr. told me the first job I would have with this company would be the Rush show, I couldn't believe it. I would see Rush, eat free, and get paid $12 per hour to help with the band's setup and breakdown!

In 1997, Rush was doing the "Test for Echo" tour, and the outdoor venue in Phoenix was the Desert Sky Pavilion. We arrived early in the day, and to no surprise, so did the band. We were like extras on a film crew. It was fascinating to see this big concert getting set up with all the tools, ramps, doorways, and more. The band had nearly a dozen trucks. That's a lot of unloading. Our crew was pushing cases in an assembly-line fashion. That I could be onstage and watch it all unfold made it even more enjoyable.

At a certain point our Roadrunner Staging group was gathered, and the drum tech was to pick one person to help him set up and polish the drum kit—as in Neil Peart's drum kit. If you know progressive-rock drumming, you know who Neil Peart is. Playing drums is a huge part of my life, and he is my absolute favorite drummer. This was an exciting moment for me. Unfortunately, drum tech guy randomly and unwittingly picked the wrong person, some guy with zero drum knowledge. I was disappointed because it was the chance of a lifetime. The guy even received a pair of Neil's used sticks after the show.

This episode included a moment in which drum tech guy, who had seen that I was observing, asked me to do him a favor. I excitedly responded with "yeah of course." He snarled, "take a hike." It was a crushing moment, and when Mike Jr. saw me, he could tell I was embarrassed. It just goes to show that certain personality types can make their way into any setting, even one as momentous as this. Several regular crew members confessed I wasn't the only person to have felt drum tech guy's needle.

Alex Lifeson, Rush's guitarist, was there early in the day, making sure the sound for his guitar was dialed in. I was allowed to be on the stage off to the right while Rush sound checked, which was unbelievable.

The afternoon settled down a little before the show. We had a superb dinner. Mike Jr. and I went wandering the grounds behind the stage. I caught a glimpse of bassist and vocalist Geddy Lee on the phone. It was just Mike Jr. and me, so Geddy was gracious and welcoming when I approached him, expressing I was a fan and that I loved Rush. It was a quick meeting, no autographs or photos—just a simple handshake from a hand that was surprisingly soft after decades of jamming on thick-gauge strings.

I had seen Neil Peart as well but wasn't aware of it because he was wearing all motorcycle gear with a helmet on. He had been riding his motorcycle from show to show while on tour. It would have been a sociable situation had I known it was him. Looking back on it now, it's better that I didn't approach. The moment would have turned me into an idiot.

Another highlight of working on the show was the all-access pass. This allowed us to go anywhere we wanted in the crowd, which was great because there were so many good spots for seeing the show. Rush no longer had an opening act, so they played two fifteen song sets. It was a phenomenal time. They even left us all with black "Test for Echo" tour t-shirts! Of course, none were available in medium, my size, but what did I care?

Working at a concert usually means a super-long day. After all of the action and excitement of setup and performance, tearing down after a show has zero appeal. That aside, this would prove to be the best first day on the job I've ever had.

I saw the Rush show again a few months later when I was back in Chicago. Afterward, my friends Lee and Sam accompanied me down to the front of the stage. We spotted drum tech guy and heckled him. The rest of the crew on hand was laughing as well.

The next gig, and unfortunately my last one with Roadrunner Staging, would be an even bigger concert with a larger stage and more trucks. U2 was on tour with the album *Pop.* They were scheduled for a sold-out show at Sun Devil Stadium in Tempe, a college football stadium seating almost 80,000 people. Roadrunner Staging was a small group of locals hired as extra hands. The workers for the show wore color-coded shirts assigned by the main crew. Ours were black, and again, none were available as medium. It included a great food buffet (after everyone else ate).

U2 had thirty trucks, and there was no floating around as at the Rush show. The road crew put you on one task, and you stood there and did it.

It was a fantastic show. U2 had a big lemon that opened into a mirror ball that the band entered from and exited into. It featured a revolutionary use of video screens, which I witnessed being built in front of my eyes. The huge main screen had dozens of square panels equipped with little pixel lights, making it the first LED screen to be used for concerts. The whole stage went from one side of the field to the other, and the screen ran right along with it. There was nothing in between. It was a great show, but we weren't allowed all-access this time. We were assigned seats we did not want to stay in, so we wandered.

Seeing a show of this caliber being set up and broken down gave me an eye-opening perspective on the work involved. I could understand why the work is accompanied by stressed-out gripers in need of a beer. People on crews like this can be unpleasant. One thing is for sure: When you see the way concerts should be run and the need for proper security, you start to understand the lack of patience that the event staff usually have.

On that note, you were expected to be sober while working a show; drinking alcohol was forbidden (if they could catch you). Most people valued such work, so they didn't risk it.

I wish I had more to add to this chapter, which is a tough one to top. If ever blue jeans were a part of the uniform, it's backstage at a concert. But unfortunately, I didn't get any more concert gigs, and I had to return to general labor ads in the paper.

Chapter 30

Hot Wax Valet

Tempe, Arizona, 1997

- Valet /amateur saboteur
- Total income: unknown

I was near Tempe, and sure enough, I found a small start-up valet company. The owner was organized, fair, and honest. He provided me with a uniform shirt requiring black shorts (which I had) and had me start at a Scottsdale restaurant with a crew of other trainees. They were all so friendly, which was new to me. Many Chicago valets could be "tough guys."

Compared with the mini-marathons I ran in Chicago, it was a cakewalk from the lot to the restaurant front. The owner saw me demonstrate the big three of valet service: *always run, open doors, don't lose keys.* He gave me an account at a Bennigan's restaurant that offered free, optional valet service. The valet stand was at the entrance of a ramp to a multi-level parking structure. This gave us strategic command of parking spaces and opportunities to park cars for tips. It was a sweet gig. There was a day guy, and I relieved him at night. It was close enough to downtown Tempe that I could ride my bike in on a lovely desert trail now covered by Tempe Town Lake. The college town was filled with nightlife and bar hopping.

I made good money working solely for tips. The owner let me keep all I earned. Even though the valet service was free, some customers didn't tip! I couldn't believe it. I hadn't yet learned the motto I would later adopt: For everyone who doesn't tip, someone else usually makes up for it.

Even though I was an experienced valet who knew how to hustle to get tips (and I did), I became increasingly frustrated when people out to dinner didn't tip. I should have just let it go, but after a few times, I started charging people $2 if they didn't tip. I unknowingly charged the restaurant owner. He fired Hot Wax Valet the next day.

I felt terrible. The owner of Hot Wax valet was a good guy, and I lost an account for him. When he told me the account was gone, I was extremely apologetic and realistic about not even asking to remain under his employment. I offered to visit the restaurant and let them know that I was responsible, but he was quite annoyed with me, and I could tell there was nothing to be done. My actions had directly affected others who counted on and worked hard for that account. My narrow perspective had gotten the better of me. Just because I may have felt insulted didn't mean I should have taken matters into my own hands.

I decided take the general labor tour back to Illinois. The timing was perfect because Phoenix was getting too hot for me, SNOWBIRD!

Chapter 31

Klein Hardware

Chicago, Illinois, 1997
- Stock/delivery/hardware consultant
- Total income: $2,226.00

Dave Bon (Chapter 21) and I found a spacious two-bedroom apartment below my brother Greg's in Chicago's Bucktown. We could even set up band practice in the living room. My brother Adam lived nearby as well.

I loved the apartment and being near my brothers. Dave continued to run Paramount Parking from the apartment. My black pants, shorts and I could resume valet parking with him while I job searched.

Re-equipped with well-known free gazette *The Chicago Reader*'s general labor section, an ad for delivery, moving, and retail help in one position initiated my in-store application. Back then, many ads were placed requesting "apply in person." It seemed like a decent supplement to any valet shifts I picked up while Dave continued to run Paramount Parking.

It was a simple interview, and work experience was all it took to qualify. They were looking for people who could manage simple tasks and become responsible self-starters.

Klein Hardware was a family-run business in the True Value franchise on Southport Avenue with lots of foot traffic. Condominiums were sprouting up in the area referred to as Wrigleyville (because of its proximity to the Chicago Cubs' home, Wrigley Field). They had a box truck and made all kinds of deliveries and repairs. We had a rear area where we cut glass, fixed screen doors, and more. These tasks required the proper tools, workspace, and the ability to transport. I learned quite a few hardware tricks and minor repairs. I re-stocked and re-merchandised because many customers never put items back after deciding not to buy. I'm guilty of it too.

I took advantage of my employee discount and rode my bike to work, which was better than driving. Even if I managed to find parking at work, trying to stop anywhere on my way home meant another jungle hunt for parking.

While I was hired full-time, they sometimes left me off the schedule because of a lack of business. I can't blame them. Besides, I could still pick up valet shifts with Paramount Parking. It was fantastic having weekends off.

Klein Hardware was a cool blue jean job. The people were great. They were laid-back about casual yet presentable attire. I didn't have to be worried about ruining my blue jeans on the job. I liked that I could go out after work and not have to change pants.

It was good to be employed while keeping my wider search active. Persistence was about to pay off with a callback for a job I'd been repeatedly applying for.

Chapter 32

Guitar Center

Chicago, Illinois, 1997–99

- Drum department sales ninja
- Total income: $26,509.57

When I moved back to Chicago, playing drums became a significant part of my life. Naturally, like any musician, I would shop at Guitar Center. There weren't many locations, so going to one was a rare treat. Uniquely, Guitar Center was divided into five departments: guitars, drums, keyboards, accessories, and pro audio. Another appeal was that customers could try out the merchandise. That's all it took to stand apart: Let people play the stuff. It got loud in there too!

I frequented the location on Chicago's north side at Clark Street and Belmont Avenue. The store had once been a tiny movie theatre. I often inquired about employment there. I kept applying as the squeaky wheel pursuing the oil. If you persist and follow up, you'll eventually get someone's attention.

After filling out several applications without a response, I asked to see a manager I could hand my completed application to. Providing it in person is advantageous. The assistant manager assured me he would get my application to the store sales manager.

I got a call later offering an interview the next day. They needed proper staffing for Christmas. One of the drum-department salesmen suggested that I wear a suit for which I had never done before. Something about wearing a suit says, "I deserve this job."

The interview was basic, but the manager tried to make it seem more official than it really was. What I know now, I think he would have preferred just to ask if I had a pulse and spoke English, but he didn't want to scare me off with such a quick screening. They desperately needed help with the drum department.

I was hired to the drum department shortly after my interview and remember feeling overwhelmed by working in that old building. The drum department was in the basement of an old city building and had a low ceiling. Nooks and crannies were filled to the gills with drum sets' parts. It was an inventory nightmare. I had yet to learn about the sales numbers the location was generating and what had to be done to achieve them.

The store rented a building down the street for storage. Imagine trying to locate a drum kit in another building and then pushing it on a cart down a snowy alley to the back of the store. The kit components had to be double-checked at the front door on the customer's way out. The Guitar Center location rented a few spots in a public pay-to-park lot half a block away, so you had to make sure the entire ticket was accounted for before you had someone pull up and double park.

Each department was able to keep its own manager, except for drums. The managers of the store hadn't deemed their current drum sales staff worthy. Sales was a two-shift operation. The closers were usually single nightlife types who might have been in a band. Openers were mostly family guys. I closed.

Guitar Center was super busy, and the salespeople were competitive. Any customer I talked to was often someone else's "guy," meaning they'd sold them merchandise in the past and now felt entitled to any future sales to that customer. This would make for challenging sales, considering anyone walking through the door was theoretically already claimed. Recognizing that context, I asked Guitar Center sales staff outside the drum department to introduce me as the new drum guy to their customers. This would be my preemptive strike on unclaimed territory. I knew that the other sales departments wanted to avoid dealing with the drum department's noise and low profit margins.

Most non-drum sales staff maintained the mantra "I'm not a drum guy." This statement implied the sale was a pass-off: It's yours.

I still recall one of those memorable guitar sales characters named Dave Hernandez, aka "Lefty." He had a ponytail and was the coolest coworker. Everyone liked him. He had a humorous, ongoing feud with our store manager. Lefty was a vintage Les Paul specialist and consistently one of the top two most successful salespeople in guitar sales: He closed deals. He lived in Roscoe Village and drove a four-door tan Grenada. He is still one of my closest LLFs. We've experienced a lot of life's shifting winds together as two partying freeloaders packed full of sarcasm and jokes.

One time Lefty pranked me good. I had placed the cash register drawer on top of the counter instead of putting it into the register and pushing it closed. I walked across the showroom, and he hid the cash drawer from me when I wasn't looking. I returned to the counter and didn't notice for a few minutes. When I did, I freaked out. After some mad searching, I saw him laughing behind one of the glass walls that separated departments. I never left cash out after that.

My customer-relations skills grew in that first winter. I had the job down, including computer use. My employee number was 009273, meaning I was the 9,273rd person that Guitar Center had hired, and it was like rank. You were often put in your place by a coworker who would say, "Yeah, what's your number?" This would imply that you needed to work there longer to know what you were talking about.

The computer system was called POS, which should have stood for "piece of shit," although it was handy if used correctly. You could check messages and review both purchase histories and nationwide numbers. This was before email became universal.

There was a lot of inside vernacular to master. "Wanking" was when any person would play butchered versions of songs with zero intention of buying. There were people who would sit down and start playing loud regardless of anyone or anything else, as if they were in a private practice space. If I was engaged in a transaction with a legitimate developing sale, and I was being blasted by a cranked amp or a car-crash drum fill, I had no problem shutting down the wanker. Wanking was why most non-drums staff despised setting foot in the department. Saturdays featured particular torture.

Another common term was "shitbag." This ultimate insult is self-explanatory. "Burning" meant you were working open to close. Even worse was the "unexpected burning" when you were asked to close after you'd opened. Someone who burned always garnered sympathy. A few burns in one week could make you crazy.

A customer was "grinding" you if they were pressuring you to give a discount. It was a daily challenge. Sometimes, I played clueless and pretended to not understand what they wanted. Once, I informed a customer who insisted on such a low price that it required getting hired and use of his employee discount. Another time, a customer was grinding me so pathetically that I finally asked, "Do you tell the grocery store what you'll pay after they ring you up?" "Dropping your pants" was another Guitar Center-ism meaning someone "grinded" a discount that was too large.

Remembering a first name often made a customer "your guy." It took a lot of work to keep repeat customers in your lane. If they came in when you weren't there, they used another salesperson. Customers were not loyal. You might spend a lot of time researching and preparing a merchandise offer for a customer who didn't complete the sale. Then, that same customer would come in on your day off and close the same deal with another salesperson. It wasn't a total loss, though. Your card file could prove you did the work, so you had an equal claim on the sale. We constantly had to reroll a deal, which meant returning the full sale amount for store credit. The credit was then used to make the sale again and split the commission between the two salespeople. It was disastrous.

One month, I was number one in sales nationwide, but my commission check was so low I realized the time and effort spent on earning commission wouldn't be worth it. I opted for base pay. After my starting probation period, I had a $1,200 monthly salary.

Most employees worked in the department of an instrument they played, but others crossed departments as well. Eben was hired in accessories within a week of my arrival. Eben mentioned he played drums, and they promptly moved him. It was harder to staff drums than accessories. Eben and I worked together in drums for a long time and were the store manager's go-to guys. The other drum personnel had all left.

We later found out that we were moving to a new location. Guitar Center was taking over the lease on a building next to the same Chernin's Shoes from which Paramount Parking had rented the parking lot for its Halsted accounts. Guitar Center had a grand-opening team that traveled the country assisting brand-new stores and prepping them to open, and they were going to re-launch our store. Some "old school" traditionalists—including both employees and customers—can always be expected to oppose such a move. I've always wondered why people are OK with being outdated. I'm not. This move meant free, spacious parking, more warehousing space, and other things necessary for our jobs. One drawback of the move was that sales staff would no longer be able to wear blue jeans.

We still had to run the existing store while operations were moving to the new building. The idea was to sell as much current inventory as possible before transferring it. They brought us all in for a preview. *A note to employers:* Do something like that when you are opening or remodeling a location. Getting a collective first glimpse of what we would be occupying and contributing to motivated us. Guitar Center closed for one full week before the grand opening so the grand-opening team could focus on the move and prepare the new site. It was a big project.

The opening was a big event, and Paramount Parking was hired to handle the parking. The new store was stunning. The drum department was in the back with its own warehouse entrance. This was good. We had our own uninterrupted corner of the warehouse. It was so spacious that all of our merchandise only took up half of our storage space and became our drum guy quick-break area. Our inventory skyrocketed.

The new location meant longer operating hours. Saturdays were now split between store openers and closers. Saturdays began with a morning meeting full of complaints about random work-related things. I preferred closing on Saturdays because that meant skipping the morning meeting.

Eben and I were the same age, and we often held the same sales numbers, ranking in the top twenty for drums nationwide. Eventually, we shared large deals because we both worked with the same customers. Eben and I were the only two drum department salespeople, and we each had to work six days a week with one day off during the week. We both had to pull a burn on the other's day off. It was nice whenever a third salesperson joined us. One person made a difference, especially on a Saturday.

Whenever a "third guy" was interviewed, Eben and I would be introduced. I always found out right away if the interviewee was a smoker. Their habit didn't sway my decision, but my inquiry kept me aware.

At one point I came up with the non-smoker's smoke break. A manager once asked me why I was outside while a fellow third drum guy who took regular smoke breaks was overwhelmed with customers inside. I said I was taking a non-smoking break. I offered to hold my hand close to my mouth like I was taking a drag, but he just walked off.

I got along with each of the third guys who joined the department because I was good at training. I knew the gear. When we didn't have a third guy, one of the advantages was never having a rotating 60-minute front door–duty shift checking receipts and incoming gear. The top salesperson could usually avoid this task. However, it was a nice break occasionally. Plus, when I did rarely work the front door, I was duty-bound to greet any female who entered.

Since we're on the topic of tasks, Guitar Center had a revolving schedule for cleaning their public restrooms. Male employees were supposed to clean the men's restroom, and one of the managers or female employees took care of the women's. I don't know how bad it got for the women's restroom, but the men's restroom, like many, could get gross. During my two year tenure, I dodged cleaning that nasty men's restroom!

Guitar Center did what we referred to as "street buys." Selling used gear was profitable and, at the time, preferable. There was no internet, so we had the cornered market for used gear. There was just one rule when buying gear for resale: DO NOT OVERPAY. The idea was to double whatever we paid for it. A lot of customers thought drums from their youth were worth more than we offered. Customers would play off different employees as well. Plenty of times, I said, "No, we are not paying that much for a used snare drum." Then, when I came in after my day off, I find the same used snare drum on our sales floor because a new person "dropped their pants."

A competing store often would call and price match whatever we were quoting on an item to satisfy their in-store customer. One particular drum salesperson had made a name for himself selling gear for different music shops all over Chicagoland. He had a distinctive voice, so I knew it was him when he called Guitar Center once for a price match.

His shtick was to ask me the price and, when I told him, to have me repeat it while on his speaker phone so his customer could hear. At first, I said the sale price was $129. When he asked me to repeat it once on his speaker, I said $99. He immediately hung up. He called back later that day saying what I did wasn't cool. I laughed and told him he was ridiculously delusional if he thought I would knowingly help him compete against us!

Another memorable character among the many customers frequenting our department—one I still remember—is Dale, whom I had met at the Clark Street store. Dale was a man with intellectual disabilities, lived with his grandmother, and took public transportation.

Dale made occasional purchases, using the layaway option for every one of them. We were always accommodating, patient, and willing to let him spend time in the drum department. Customers noticed and often complimented us on how we treated Dale.

He had put a drum set on layaway and made payments a few bucks at a time for months. He often talked about the day he would pick it up. On one random Friday, a massive snowstorm had blown in the night before, and the blizzard-like conditions weren't letting up. I lived close and rode public transportation to work, which was the only option among three feet of snow. There weren't many customers that day, so the staff were all taking it easy with minimal work.

Then, who walked in? Dale! He was layered up, dripping wet, covered in snow, and tracking it behind him. When on a mission, some people can't be deterred by an inconvenience such as snowstorm, and Dale was one of them. This wasn't the typical visit to make a payment and ask random questions. He was there to pick up his drum set!

His drums had been sold at a discount because they were floor models, which are out of boxes and assembled. I asked him how he would get the drums home, and he said he was taking the bus. If you know anything about drums, you're aware they include a lot of components. They are collectively heavy and awkward, and there's no way a bus—especially a city bus—will sit at a stop while you load them in from three feet of snow and then have nowhere to put them once you're on the bus. I couldn't imagine him achieving this on a warm, sunny day, much less in a Chicago snowstorm.

I went in to see our store manager and I explained that Dale wanted to take the drum set home on two different buses. Our manager hung his head and sighed. There was no way we could let Dale take the drums without a proper way to transport them, and hearing this from the store manager made it a lot easier for Dale to understand.

I called Dale's grandmother and explained the situation. It was one of those moments when compassion overrides complying with the customer's wish. Bringing those drums home meant so much to

Dale. Later that week, their pastor was able to pick them up with the church van, and Dale was finally able to have his drums.

Eventually, Eben and I decided it was time for a bump in salary from $1,200 monthly to $1,600. Our manager had no problem with that adjustment for not having to worry about an entire department. We got our raise with a simple meeting.

We managed ourselves in the drum department the entire time I worked at Guitar Center. It was nice. Management sometimes wandered the floor looking for staff who weren't busy and said, "Get on those phones."

Lesson: *Phones are valuable tools that can deter many problems.* I adopted the Fake-It Maneuver. Whenever I saw a manager, I picked up the phone and pretended to be deep in conversation with a customer. I discovered I could do the same for lingerers on the sales floor that keep looking for attention and won't go away with no purchase intent. Pretend you're on the phone. Occasionally, if I was working at the store entrance and saw a customer pestering drum guys, I would call the drum counter and keep them on the phone faking business talk to bail them out.

Another function of the phones was paging other departments but leaving them wondering who did it. The source of a page prompted a few in-store investigations. If you were sly, your pages were unidentifiable. Phones were used for store-closing announcements, which were always fun. It's funny how some customers get upset when the store is closing and they're asked to leave. If you're not buying anything, see you next time! You could usually tell what kind of day other employees had by how they made their closing page. I developed my own craft—so much that coworkers often watched the clock for the fifteen minutes before closing and had me announce last call for purchases.

If you got good at closing, you were already prepared to leave. The closing crew left together to reinforce personal safety and keep one person from staying behind with unfinished work. It's a good policy. One person alone shouldn't close a store like that at night—too much coveted merchandise, some of it very expensive. I always had my department ready to go and then wound up waiting around. The closing hours got slap-happy and led to a lot of time-burning jokes and silliness. I used to walk into the warehouse and yell, "This is bullshit!" It became its own type of tradition.

The company held annual training seminars. I was sent to California to visit three major drum equipment manufacturers, DW, REMO, and Roland. It was an enjoyable, all-expenses-paid time away from the store. I learned several things that helped me better sell gear. Another time, they sent me out of state to open and train a new Guitar Center's drum department. I built the same displays as we had done at our store. After this trip, I became the department manager for drums.

I was diligent and particular about inventory. On my watch, our inventory counts went from disastrous to accurate. Drums finally had everything tagged with the proper SKU numbers and signs. Making signs takes talent and attention to detail. You must be consistent and accurate because customers will use "the sign says" to grind for a lower price.

Being the manager didn't mean greater income unless the department made a certain amount beyond what it paid in salary. My bonus never happened, and it became clear that Guitar Center would not hold a meaningful future for me.

By the time I was two years into the job, I was a veteran, we had all new managers, and most people I'd started with left. I made friends with a new circuit of employees. However, the store and its vibe had changed. Sometimes, you don't realize the nostalgia of something until it's gone. Times were shifting as the century ended. The growing internet was impacting work, and buying used gear from a retail store started becoming a bit more *passé.*

I gave a simple two-week notice to the store manager stating I was interested in pursuing music, something no Guitar Center manager ever wanted to hear. Thankfully, Paramount Parking was still hanging on, and working for Dave three to four days a week again had appeal. Paramount was an excellent continuing option because I wouldn't have to "find a job" at once.

I learned so much about drum gear and customer service at Guitar Center. It taught me not to overpay for gear or buy crap gear ever again. A job like that can make you a better customer too. Other memorable highlights at Guitar Center were the clinics they hosted featuring drummers such as Jason Bonham, Mike Portnoy, and Billy Cobham. I discovered that drummers are communal. Have you ever heard of a guitar circle? Probably not.

Then of course there was the issue of what was worn on the legs. Initially, the old-school environment at the first Guitar Center location on Belmont was spared from the company's blue jean ban. The opening of the new store on Halsted instituted the current company look. It did not include blue jeans.

Chapter 33

Eli-Wyn Upholstery

Chicago, Illinois, 1999
- Delivery driver/shop help/neglecter of antiques
- Total income: $9,902.00

A wonderful thing about not needing a job immediately is that you can be picky about your next one. There is a sense of calm, control, and self-reliance when you go to an interview you're not desperate about. The *Chicago Reader* advertised for a furniture-delivery driver under my trusted General Labor section.

The employers were a married couple. I'll refer to them as Mr. and Mrs. Furniture. My interview was with Mrs. Furniture. She was a delightful woman. My personality, experience, and valid driver's license was all that was needed to qualify me for delivery driver.

They ran Eli-Wyn Upholstery in partnership with a high-end furniture shop they had in Lincoln Park. Many upholstery customers came from this store, and the two businesses complemented each other nicely.

The upholstery shop was within walking distance of my home in a building that housed a vast freight elevator that led exclusively to their entrance on the second floor. This elevator access was priceless. The upholsterers worked at large square tables. Lesson: *You can take on any project with a large square worktable.*

A fifteen-passenger van with the seats removed allowed for multiple couch-loading of many sizes. I was off on Saturdays and Sundays, thank God. Driving in Chicago on a Saturday is madness. Traffic always sucks, and there's never anywhere to park a large van.

Delivering reupholstered furniture and new couches can be tricky. Logistical drop-off points were consistently overlooked details when customers scheduled deliveries.

Once, we delivered a reupholstered couch up three floors to an apartment with no elevator. It was an older piece with thin metal legs we didn't remove. We put a lot of holes in the drywall and never said anything. I always knew to remove the legs because that eliminates many mistakes. A few weeks later, Mrs. Furniture showed me pictures of the notably dinged-up walls. This was my first significant screw-up. I should have told her when it happened.

They wanted me to be available for deliveries, but that often meant being on the clock with no deliveries scheduled. On one slow day, I was organizing the Eli-Wyn location that served as the main warehouse. Turning couches upright on its side was typical for storing. While our side-stacking technique was generally OK, it was *not appropriate for handmade antiques.* Mr. Furniture had a vintage couch at the shop for upholstery work. It was a beautiful carved frame made from one piece of wood with horses smoothly detailed into the glossy armrests. I had placed a padded moving blanket on the ground before turning this piece on its side, which ground down one of the horses. The damage was considerable. I didn't even know I'd done it.

Later, Mr. Furniture mentioned the damage, and I denied it. I didn't remember it at first, but later I did and was too stubborn to admit it. After this (incident number two), I knew something was brewing. I could feel a change in the air. Pending termination was on the horizon, so I started job searching.

A friend alerted me to an employment opportunity. I interviewed for it on a Wednesday, and they wanted me to start the following Monday. Eli-Wyn deserved notice, so I had a serious dilemma!

I went to work at Eli-Wyn the following Thursday morning, and Mr. Furniture was waiting for me at the time clock. I knew the fix was in because Mrs. Furniture wasn't around. Still, I was prepared for the situation I was about to face. He asked me not to clock in and wanted to talk in the other room. He was being pleasant and laying down his reasons. I could tell he had planned out what he wanted to say. So, I let him get it all out while I contained the joy of my existing backup.

I responded to his request to find another job with a simple OK. That was all I said during a conversation in which I was fired. It felt worse for them than it did for me, because as I was leaving, a teary-eyed Mrs. Furniture met me at the door. She hugged me and wished me luck. I even uttered the old "it'll be fine, everything happens for a reason."

I felt relieved as I busted out the first-floor metal warehouse door with a John Travolta strut down Webster Street on a sunny, warm December day. With my two-week notice dilemma resolved, I would start the next chapter on Monday. Losing a job with one lined up is a fine feeling indeed—among the best we may encounter in our working lives.

I was a willful worker in my twenties. I would have liked to have made a better situation with Eli-Wyn. They were honest and fair. They didn't deserve to be put in that situation. I did a respectable job, but I was careless. A few critical mistakes and my lack of concern for the damage I caused were justifiable reasons to let me go.

I liked this job. I learned that any couch with springs is a good piece of furniture. I could drive all over Chicago while running errands and stop at home on a slow day for lunch.

About the pants: These kinds of blue jean–wearing delivery jobs have always appealed to me because they represent a casual environment, which Eli- Wyn was. Delivery jobs usually require a uniform or work pants I'm not inspired to pay for. I was just delivering the stuff, man—not reupholstering it.

Chapter 34

Jeff McClusky
and Associates

Chicago, Illinois, 1999–2001

- Personal assistant and recycling pioneer
- Total income: $38,858.48

My friend managed a five story building in Wicker Park four blocks from my apartment. She recommended me for an open position seeking a temporary office assistant with Jeff McClusky and Associates (JMA), an independent promotion business that rented the entire second level.

The CEO, Jeff McClusky, needed a third personal assistant to do his Christmas shopping. Jeff already had two long-term assistants, one personal and one administrative. I had a simple interview and got the job by telling JMA I could start right away and verifying that I had an insured vehicle.

The business was tricky to describe because independent promotion can mean many things. In JMA's case, they were a major music industry player with a corner on the music-promo market, and they were just a few blocks from my home!

The entire office was decorated with autographed record awards from major acts in the music industry. Jeff had met them all and owned the pictures to prove it. JMA had become a stopping point for entertainers in Chicago. It was a comfortable place with a central conference room for business meetings, performances, and meet-and-greets.

Even though this job was *walking distance* from my apartment, I still had to use my four-door Plymouth for shopping. I didn't mind. The job had come at the right time, and JMA compensated me for mileage and gas.

My primary responsibility was "whatever Jeff needed." He rarely relayed instructions to anyone other than his two immediate assistants. The forty-five other staff members accustomed to a holiday assistant knew they could keep me busy with office errands as well.

It was an incredible job! I had a credit card for purchases. My day began with Jeff's requests scribbled on an extra-long yellow notepad. I bought pricey handbags, video game systems, team jerseys, concert tickets, gift cards, and anything else new and hip. I did all the shopping and deliveries. JMA provided me with a Nokia pea green–screen cell phone, which was nice. Cell phone technology was still new and uncommon at the century's turn. No camera, GPS, or web browser yet—just a mobile phone with T9!

It was a crazy December. Fortunately, my valet parking experience helped. I spent a lot of time on Michigan Avenue, where I found loading areas that were legal "30-minute parking zones." Unfortunately, I got towed twice that month. There is no place closer to hell in this world than a city tow yard.

In addition to my Christmas shopping, I would run daily to Starbucks to get Jeff's order of sixteen Grande decaffeinated whipped cappuccinos, lightly skimmed and double cupped. On Fridays, I made the trip again in the afternoon, making it thirty-two total coffees. Jeff drank (possibly scooped) all thirty-two over his long weekend at the office.

When my temporary Christmas employment ended on December 24, I received a bonus as well as gift cards. After a month of my above-and-beyond dedicated work, JMA came to rely on me and decided to hire me full-time for one of my all-time favorite jobs! If you apply yourself and maximize your value, you can make your place in the working world. I did just that.

My tenure at JMA was filled with music industry guests and courtesy lunches from record management companies. This included a lot of post-meal cleanup and, for me, ample, tasty leftovers. Everyone in the music industry wanted to do business with JMA.

One of the many special guests who came in was Red Rocker Sammy Hagar promoting his 50th birthday tour. This was a big deal for me. I'd been a fan since seeing the video for "I Can't Drive 55" and all through the Van Halen years (and after). Coincidentally, I was wearing a solid-red shirt when we met.

Bon Jovi was making a comeback with their new album *Crush,* and they did a stop at our office on the tour. JMA brought in Famous Dave's ribs. I spent most of the time in the kitchen area. No one was with me when their guitarist, Richie Sambora, came looking for food. I got up to assist him with his beverage, figuring he would return to the conference room with everyone else. Instead he sat down at my table and ate with me. This was a moment when many people might get nervous, but it seemed like he just wanted to eat in peace, away from the chaos in the other room. So we ate ribs together. I remember telling him I played in a local band and how we struggled to find the right bass player. He sympathized, claiming finding the right bass player can be a lifelong search, even for Bon Jovi.

John Mayer had just released a remastered version of his debut album, *Room for Squares.* It had been a hit for him, and it was getting much attention. He performed acoustically in our conference room one day. I learned he was touring and looking for a drummer, so I emailed him. He responded, asking me to send a demo. I never did—I didn't have one and didn't bother to put forth the effort to make one, which was a big mistake. I was working there for an opportunity like this! I should have learned his album from start to finish and dropped a demo off in person at the Tennessee address. My life might have turned out completely different if I'd had the vision.

JMA hosted Shakira, Michelle Branch, Tesla, the Go-Go's, Anastasia, Christina Millan, Nelly Furtado, Pete Yorn, Josh Homme and Nick Oliveri from Queens of the Stone Age, and even Mr. Cub, Ernie Banks!

One of the best benefits at JMA was getting tickets or VIP passes to any show I wanted. I'd look through the paper for shows I wanted to see, and that was it—free access to any show I wanted! My roommate and I often benefited from Jeff's season tickets right behind the Chicago Bulls' bench.

I worked nine to five Monday through Friday but often stayed later. Most of the office was cleared out by five, so the after-hours solitude was nice. I had a key to the front door and was trusted with running daily business. I further frequented a photoshop where Jeff had pictures developed weekly. If I had my own film to develop, they comped me for it. This was before the digital-camera revolution.

I used FedEx Ground for all local deliveries and cleared out a closet I deemed "shipping and receiving." I saved thousands of dollars by reusing packing and shipping materials. Others who worked there appreciated my initiative and complied with my requests to re-purpose packing and shipping items.

I began giving rides to guests and staff members. Jeff's old Mercedes, a nicer vehicle, stayed in the parking garage and was used to chauffeur music industry executives. JMA had many demands and had grown to rely on me, so they bought a company vehicle. They traded Jeff's Mercedes for a used four wheeled drive vehicle so that I could do my job effectively in a snowy, cold-weather city such as Chicago. It was perfect. Once I had that, I did it all. I was the Office Driver.

The company vehicle was kept in a designated, heated spot at the office building's underground parking garage. It was awesome not to scrape snow and ice off the car! I was allowed to keep my motorcycle in that garage. It may have been three and a half blocks away, but a secure, heated garage with an automatic door was worth it!

Employees who'd been brought on like me as an assistant had eventually moved up to either promotional salesperson or an assistant assigned directly to one. I had started at $10 per hour, was now making $12 per hour, and was yet to ascend another rung. The new CFO made it clear that my pay wasn't increasing.

Even though I'd worked at JMA for two years, my role was at a dead end. As time went on, I increasingly established that I didn't want to promote any music that I didn't like. I was becoming aware that my particular assistant position wasn't one designed to grow or to last.

A major event would soon make such aspects not matter. Everything came to a screeching halt when two planes collided into the World Trade Center towers on September 11, 2001. I remember the day vividly. JMA took a hit from that tragic event since so much of our business included air travel. JMA started making cutbacks.

One morning, I came to work and the mood in the air was tense, which was rare at JMA. When I heard about the layoffs, I knew it was just a matter of time. After lunch, they sat me down and closed the door, and I let them say what they had worked out. I was in a familiar place: I knew what was coming. They offered me severance, which I accepted. People were crying a lot that day.

In the end, there were three rounds of layoffs. The fact that I was in the first round was no surprise. I mean, I had turned a job meant to last three weeks into two years! Who was I kidding, even pretending to be upset? By then I knew my abilities. I would find work. It was a different story for others, however. The layoffs were wounds to their careers.

I got a call later that day from Jeff's admin assistant, checking to see how I was doing. I responded that I had just gotten home from an interview and would start my new job the following Monday! Her voice perked up—she seemed both happy and relieved. My good fortune had provided some light on a dark day of firing people.

I learned that certain jobs are a daily treat and that I should be grateful for them. I was reminded again that not everything lasts. Every day at an excellent job should be enjoyed! The most important thing I learned from this job was that opportunities continued surrounding my life. I had more chances to meet people, discover new music, and understand how to promote music. Opportunity knocks when and where it wants; it's my duty to be ready to answer. With JMA I made many great friends and shared countless shows. If you didn't wear blue jeans to this job, well, you just weren't rock and roll!

Chapter 35

Lemmings Bar

Chicago, Illinois, 2001–02

- Door dude/bar-back snake
- Total income unknown

While employed at JMA, I had started working at a bar called Lemmings that I lived across the street from but went in sporadically. I didn't like the smell of cigarettes glued to my clothes, so I typically limited my hang-out time in bars.

Lemmings didn't have live music or food, but it was a cool place with a good crew of friendly bartenders and door staff, accompanied by a pleasant selection of bottled beers. Closing was at 2 a.m. on weekdays and 3 a.m. on Saturdays. Lemmings needed a second guy to work at the door on Saturday nights, so I talked to a bartender about the job and he had me shadow the Friday-night door guy. The bar was so close that I could see inside it from my apartment, which supported always being on time for work. I understood it would include exposure to secondhand smoke.

Before starting, I clarified that I wasn't there to physically handle people. I wasn't a bouncer. They agreed and if there was the occasional tough guy, anyone bartending acted quickly. It was a straightforward job: Check IDs, discourage drunkards, gather empty glasses and bottles, change kegs, and bring beer from a dungy basement to restock the bar. Checking IDs is easy if you know what to look for. While I would have needed help spotting a professional-grade fake ID, checking them still deterred minors from trying to enter.

At the night's end, it was the door guy's responsibility to wipe down ashtrays. I refused to do this, which turned out to be fine. The staff included some smokers who didn't mind it, so I would restock beer in exchange for their cleaning the ashtrays. Bartenders would share their tips with the door personnel, and we were allowed one beer at the end of the shift. I always went with a pint. Lesson: *By going with the draft instead of the bottle, the beer can be bottomless.*

Lemmings never had dead air inside because the bartenders chose the music from behind the bar. They did have televisions, but the music was always playing.

After a while, the other door guy started bartending and the owner got a friend to work the door with me. This door guy eventually had surgery and was in a leg brace for a long time. You'd think being physically debilitated from standing would mean disqualification from employment that requires one to be on their feet. But for some reason, they decided he could solely check IDs. Picture the scene: The door guys' table is at the front door, but this one guy sits on a stool with his healing leg propped up, right in front of the entrance. It was ridiculous. How was he supposed to be the only door guy for an hour until I got there? It was simple: He couldn't. So, they changed our shifts. I now came in first, and he came in after me. Once there, he could only check IDs while I did everything else. On the plus side, I raked in extra tips because the bartenders could see and smell BS. I did though lose the opportunity to talk to the girls coming in.

In time, they had to get someone else. Enter Demon/Nacho. A JMA coworker once described a Lemmings regular and told me to call him Demon. When I first met Demon, he was puzzled about how I knew his old nickname. This was the only time I ever called him that. Demon approached me once much later, saying, "Hey man, don't call me Demon anymore. I have a new nickname." I immediately thought to myself, "I called you Demon once, as a joke, when we first met months ago and have never called you that again." But I indulged him anyway and asked, "Oh yeah, what's your new nickname?" He enthusiastically replied, "Nitro. Call me Nitro." Amused, I said, "You can't choose your own nickname. Someone else has to do that." I chuckled and shrugged him off, saying, "Dude, I'm not calling you that." When I came into work the following Saturday, people in the bar talked about a guy they called "Nacho." I didn't get it. When the bartender said "Nitro" to me sarcastically, I cracked up. Demon had been telling everyone to call him "Nitro." Someone from across the bar had mockingly asked, "Call you what? Nacho?" and it stuck. Within a week, everyone was calling him "Nacho." Fortunately, he adopted it. He just wanted a nickname. He wanted to work at Lemmings so badly that he would voluntarily collect empty glasses. Lemmings hadn't wanted to hire him; bars usually watch out for regulars who want to work in the bar. Nacho had been monitoring the incapacitated door guy/leg-brace business, and when the bar needed someone to replace him, Nacho stepped in. It turned out he'd cut down his drinking, and he became the other Saturday-night door guy.

Finally, the work was balanced. I stayed with the early start. Ideally, inside the bar-job circuit, one goes from door guy to bartender. That didn't happen for me, and it became clear it wouldn't. The theoretically vertical move on the pay scale involved currying extra favor with the bar owner, and I wasn't good at that. I didn't like the idea of contributing to a customer's drinking problem, which is what bartenders often wind up doing. Plus, at the door, I could step out of the smoke.

When I got laid off from JMA, it was great to have a backup. Being a door guy let me socialize on Saturday nights and promote my band. I liked going to a bar and coming home with more money than I'd brought. I wasn't a big party-on-Saturday-night type, anyway. Saturdays are always busy with long lines and no drink specials.

Lemmings staff and patrons were mostly blue-collar guys, musicians, and partiers. Blue jeans and a t-shirt made the proper uniform for that cakewalk job.

Chapter 36

The Feather Building

Chicago, Illinois, 2001–03

- Elevator-operator dude
- Total income: Whatever I got from discounted rent

I include this position because I was "paid" in credit for my rented rehearsal space. The Feather Building was a five-story building along railroad tracks with a direct view of Chicago's infamous skyline. The landlords lived on the fifth floor. The hours of operation for the four floors of artists space were 10 a.m. to midnight.

I started renting this space with another drummer. We had a large rectangular room with radiator heat that could easily fit the two drum sets we set up across from each other. Many other bands and artists were renting spaces as well.

We split the $400 rent and took a second-floor space because a two-flight trip with drum equipment would be more manageable if the elevator wasn't working. Plus, the first floor was more open to theft.

I was there so often the landlords approached me about helping bands use the elevator. The freight-elevator access was behind a locked door. As a result, renters were required to sign up for elevator use on a dry-erase calendar at the entrance. There was no texting back then. The system worked nicely.

I looked over the calendar and initialed whatever shifts for elevator use the landlords left open. The maximum credit they would allow was $100 off my monthly rent. I scheduled my rehearsals around my shifts, and I could access the elevator after closing for my own use.

The other renters, especially musicians, liked dealing with me because I was more flexible with load-ins. Occasionally they could come to my practice space, where I'd usually be rehearsing, knock on the door, and have me take them to the elevator.

This was a valuable experience. I had a place to socialize if I wanted to avoid going to a smoke-filled bar. There were always musicians and artists hanging out in the building.

AUDIOBON, my band with Dave Bon, became more active, and rehearsing there was not practical for the band. We found another practice space. Wearing blue jeans isn't ideal when I play drums because I constantly move my legs in sync with the timing. Shorts or loose pants work best for me, especially when in radiator heat. If I rode my bike in cold weather, I could layer shorts under nylon pants but not under jeans. I eventually just started keeping shorts at the space. I would, however, still hang the blue jean crown on my elevator guy head!

Chapter 37

Ashland Addison Florist

Chicago, Illinois, 2001–02

- Delivery individual/non-smoking outcast
- Total income: $8,405.76

So there I was, laid off from JMA and bummed out. I started job-searching that afternoon to stay confident and catch up financially. I still had my Lemmings door gig, along with AUDIOBON gigs. I saw an ad in the *Chicago Reader* General Labor section for a full-time licensed delivery driver with the magic words, vehicle provided. With my résumé ready, I biked to their shop, which was just half a block from my Feather Building practice space.

The business was Ashland Addison Florist, the largest flower-delivery service on the Chicago North Side. A family-owned business, since 1932. It had a large facility, staff, and fleet of forest-green cargo vans. Ashland Addison was used for many funeral homes and hospitals. It operated seven days a week with an effective delivery system.

It was a simple walk-in interview with the delivery manager, who hired me immediately. During initial training, I shadowed a smoker for a week. I quickly realized that delivery driver was another work category sought by cigarette smokers. They can smoke while they work! The delivery drivers often left cigs in the ashtrays—highly unpleasant for a smoke-averse employee like me.

To avoid the almost certain parking issues, it was common for drivers to have a runner for downtown deliveries. Being a runner was suitable for those who didn't have a driver's license. Driver pulls up, runner jumps out and delivers the order, and the driver stays with vehicle. Any tips were split. After my week of shadowing, I was eager to start on my own.

The manager had recently been issued a new minivan to use as a company vehicle. I could use the minivan as the only non-smoker with a safe driving record. My hours were pull-time [see Chapter 16]. I started at 8 a.m. because there were morning deliveries. I was usually done by early afternoon. Since I rode my bike, leaving with the sun still out could mean a warmer ride. The schedule allowed me to practice drums and work elevator shifts at The Feather Building.

Saturdays were half-days, and I had Sundays off. Ashland Addison had an excellent wrapping process and computer system for organizing deliveries. We had Nextel radios that operated like CBs, so the shop could easily contact a driver who was out delivering. Management tried to keep each driver in the same area every day. Mine was convenient because it was close to my apartment.

I couldn't care less about having flowers sent to me, but the deliveries made many happy. It never failed: For every delivery, numerous people would approach me and ask, "Are those for me?" After a while, I started replying, "Hmmm...let me check. Ah, yes, flowers for random stranger at this place and time." Of course I was just having fun, but some people didn't pick up on the levity. You'd be amazed at how many hopeful recipients grant entry to a guy with a clipboard and flowers. Several times, females let me into their apartments, sometimes wearing only a bathrobe!

Anything under five floors meant using the stairs, which I preferred anyway for cardio and efficiency. I learned quickly that elevators made delivery times even longer, especially when others were riding it up just one flight. I was glad to get the funeral-home route. There was no tip, but most of those deliveries were a simple drop-off at a "flower room." They did not include stairs, intruders, parking issues, or security.

Even though this was a simple delivery job, some people were better at it than others. I got the necessary info on each delivery. Getting all packages signed for and into human hands was crucial. I never had a problem approaching a recipient's neighbors to ask them to accept a package and be accountable for it. While returning to the shop with an undelivered package was not ideal, what mattered most was following the basic delivery protocol that management outlined.

Ashland Addison was so busy during the winter holidays that they held their holiday party in January. They had a fancy dinner, and I got the impression they appreciated their employees. I was awarded an acknowledgment of excellent work done. Although I'd only been with them a few months, the owner hugged me and said, "Welcome to the family." The gesture was nice, but it was too early for me to feel like kin.

There were more smokers than non-smokers at the shop, and the warehouse was the smoking room. The computers used to route and check in deliveries were stationed in that warehouse. In winter, none of the smokers went outside. Being an avid non-smoker, I shared my feelings about secondhand smoke. That might include covering my face with my shirt while at the computer. Even though they likely understood my grievances were reasonable, my stance on the issue began to make me a *persona non grata* among the smokers.

Then, I had caused considerable damage to the nice new minivan I was issued. Consequently, I had to use one of the cargo vans, which was huge and way more complicated than the smaller minivan. It meant sharing with a smoker as well. Ugh. Then, while driving impatiently on another day, I put a big dent in the front end of that cargo van. I had to inform the shop right away.

In Chicago, side damage to a delivery vehicle is understood. Front-end damage, however, implies negligent driving. With this added to my constant protest against working in secondhand-smoke clouds, the warehouse manager politely suggested I find another job. I was OK with it. They were not adopting non-smoking policies that the rest of the country was. I thanked him for giving me notice.

Being asked to find another job as opposed to being fired left me with a lingering sense of considerate professionalism on his part. But I stopped showing up after one week of a two-week notice. It just felt weird. Knowing I was walking the plank, the smokers felt even more free to overlook my comfort among them. I was glad to go.

The job taught me even more about the ins and outs of Chicago's roadways, loading zones, and parking spots. I was still working at Lemmings, and AUDIOBON was playing live shows. I'd be fine. In the end, most of us will be. We just have to keep traveling toward our peace and self-awareness in the distance on a trail without a map.

This company called for some formality of uniform; blue jeans weren't considered professional attire. Black pants and their branded shirt were required.

Chapter 38

Blum Animal Hospital

Chicago, Illinois, 2002–05

- Veterinary assistant/animal lover
- Total income: $59,890.14

In the *Chicago Reader* General Labor section, I saw an ad for a veterinary assistant. Apply in person at Blum Animal Hospital: full-time, Saturdays required, no experience necessary, and the magic words: "will train."

Blum was located directly across the street from the historic movie theatre that housed the original Guitar Center (Chapter 32). Blum Animal Hospital was started in 1952 in a typical Chicago three-story rectangle-style building.

Applying in person let me glimpse the unfamiliar business I was applying for. I received a call the next day. The woman on the phone wished to pre-interview me before scheduling an in-person interview. She had questions about my previous jobs, the dates of employment, and my availability. Many employers won't waste time with a formal interview until they know you can commit to the schedule or pass other pre-screening questions.

Lesson: *It's critical to be "on" for a phone interview and to keep your answers brief.* You want an in-person interview, so try to get off the phone before you discuss too much and give them any cause for second-guessing.

Blum scheduled an in-person interview. I made sure to approach it with proper decorum, including dressing well.

Blum Animal Hospital ran a successful veterinary practice. With three levels and innumerable doors, it was one of those facilities that just doesn't end. The second floor comprised a surgery room, a second treatment center, an isolation room, and a library/office for doctors to make calls.

The interview was lengthy. Merely having a pet while growing up didn't automatically qualify you for pet medical care. There were many "what would you do in this situation" questions. I was hired and able to start the following Monday. I knew driving to work wouldn't be an option because of the parking. It'd be either public transportation or a simple bike ride, often in extreme weather.

Saturdays would be every other week, and I would get a weekday off in exchange, an arrangement I found appealing. Because I was new, my other weekday off was Tuesday, the most undesired day. The best day was Monday, which provided a two-day weekend. My schedule with Blum relieved my need to work my door job at Lemmings, plus I'm always glad to put another smoky situation in the rear view.

Blum Animal Hospital's new hires shadowed an experienced employee for two weeks. A lot of time went into their new hires because they needed to be thorough about certain aspects some people may not have been OK with, such as euthanasia, surgery, and the sight of blood. The animal hospital performed every procedure except an MRI, so you couldn't be the least bit squeamish. Proper training was necessary because pet bites were job hazards. You had to be reliable, willing to learn, and able to work with others as well; they advocated the "team approach."

The person training you had to sign off on releasing you as ready for work. The employee I shadowed was a nice girl with a genuine love for animals. I always looked up to people like her who had genuine compassion that I lacked.

As at many Chicago businesses, the employee parking lot was off the alley in back of the hospital. For some reason the lot served as the smoking area. Some smokers smoked right outside the one entrance, which never made sense to me. Why stay so tight to the building to smoke when there's so much outdoor square footage starting a few feet away?

They had two reserved spots for the owners, Dr. Rubin and Dr. Dann. Dr Rubin was one who dove deeply into his field, building many professional relationships including Oprah Winfrey and her cocker spaniels. He served many wealthy clients who went out of their way to see him and would even wait a long time for appointments. I used to call him "Doc Hollywood" and, to coworkers, "the Rubes."

I swear Dr. Rubin could have diagnosed a pet just by touching it. He examined the most difficult pets without major restraints on them, an acquired skill. Dr. Rubin always referred to clients by their name instead of their pet's name. That eliminates confusion. You can love the pets all you want, but you must sell your service to people as Dr. Rubin did to produce Blum's numbers. It was a leading lesson in customer service.

The co-owner, Dr. Dann, was a little different. He had a solid clientele of friends, neighbors, and family. He was good at his job and always booked up. He was direct with his requests and not prone to having personal conversations with the staff, which was tough to adapt to for some.

The doctor staff was impressive. Many were formerly at farms or right out of vet school serving at their first job. There was even a holistic doctor. With seven exam rooms, they could assign a doctor to each room.

I remember being overwhelmed by the amount of activity at Blum. I could see why anyone graduating from vet school would want to work there. At the time I didn't understand how rare it was for a vet practice to have Blum's volume of business and be located in a happening, client-rich neighborhood.

Blum was different from other veterinary practices in how they referred to job titles. I was hired as a veterinary assistant, which technically was more of a kennel position. The assistant's position involved being present during procedures and services. It was helpful for the doctors to have someone who could help with properly holding and guiding pets through medical exams, X-rays, blood draws, and heart-rate monitoring.

The veterinary care coordinators (VCC's) handled the practice's administrative aspects. It was a versatile position that appealed to college students, young people finding themselves, and general admin lifers. My sister Teresa worked as a VCC for a while. That was fun working together.

Blum further had "vet tech" positions, which were more-advanced roles similar to those of a traditional vet assistant. Blum branded vet assistants could move up to vet tech and pursue a career in veterinary medicine. This made assistant another versatile position that attracted college students, young people finding themselves, and general labor lifers.

Vet techs did the tests, follow-ups, and anesthetic procedures that doctors couldn't get to. These included ANAL GLAND EXPRESSION.

The idea of expressing anal glands gave me scant joy. It was a most unpleasant and commonly requested procedure. Many times when walking through the treatment area, I'd see an assistant holding a dog for a tech who squeezed a substance from the dog's anus, emitting the foulest stench. If the substance got on you, you had to change your uniform. I would have preferred just to burn it. Hospital scrub uniforms were provided for all departments by Blum.

The maintenance aspect of vet assistant made the job "general labor." The assistant team had a manager who oversaw all scheduling and assignments. During the week, there were day and evening shifts. With a bar called Big City Tap nearby, those who worked a closing shift sometimes went out for drinks afterwards. I had an opening shift, which most people preferred but not I—it meant getting up early. Sundays were closed to the general public, but they included occasional overtime opportunities for staff. Overnight patients and boarders required one doctor and one assistant on Sundays. Sunday was always an easy day.

One day while returning an upset cat to its cage I received my first cat bite. Once the cat is in the cage and showing aggression, the last thing you do is reach in. Sure enough, I tried to pet a mad cat in its cage, and it bit me, piercing layers of skin. In addition to being excruciating, cat bites can infect your blood with toxins and require a tetanus shot and antibiotics.

I became familiar with a pair of large suede gloves that allowed for proper examining without much restraint. Some people reacted strangely when I entered the room with hawk-handling gloves, but I explained that it's safer for the cat. I just let the cat chew on an empty finger slot. The doctors never had a problem using safety equipment such as muzzles, gloves, and collars, when necessary.

One half of my shift was assigned to a doctor, which meant familiarizing myself with their schedule. Multi-tasking, time management, and attention to detail were necessary when looking over the files that each doctor would use. Assistants had to prep the exam room for appointments, escort clients to and from the rooms, and assist with pre-exam procedures such as gathering vaccinations, checking a pet's weight, collecting urine/fecal samples, and obtaining any blood work that might be needed beforehand. Understanding how the different doctors conducted exams called for working with each one for a while. The doctors preferred to be helped by the expert assistants rather than new hires or pet owners.

After some time getting good at the job, I was occasionally assigned to the practice owners, who required that their assistants be readily available nearby. When assigned to the owners, there was no expectation to be cleaning while the doctor talks with client. I would have been just fine with being assigned to the owners for both halves of my shift. Doctors looked relieved when I was their assistant.

The other half of the workday, I was a "floater." I didn't mind being a floater. It let me work alone, tend to the cats, and assist with the post-operative checkups. Many puppies and kittens were recuperating from spaying and neutering. Who wouldn't want to care for them?

Floating was a relief if I was hungover or tired. I'm an expert at finding easy work or ways to doze off on the job if I'm not feeling well. Even though I hated cleaning the bathrooms, it allowed me to sit down for five minutes. This extra time in the bathroom was when I came up with the "Tootsie Roll prank." I would slightly chew a Tootsie Roll and then place it on the toilet seat. When someone saw it, I picked it up with my bare hands.

Assistants had to be busy all the time: The old "if you have time to lean, you have time to clean." A list of responsibilities was constantly updated and revised, usually as a three-page printout.

This kept personnel busy without having to tell them what to do. The assignments were simple maintenance chores we signed off on.

Because I rode my bike to work, I was always layered under my scrubs. This allowed me to quickly assist clients with carry-outs. Even if it was cold out, a five to ten minute trip into the fresh air and away from the hospital chaos was welcome.

As I had at JMA, I made efficient use of packing and shipping materials. I became a go-to resource for moving boxes. Rather than throw boxes away, I kept many intact to repurpose them. For example, I figured out how to create a perfect storage-bin system by emptying a box containing a particular dozen bottles or tubes, folding in the flaps, and putting the product back into the box. Plus, it made inventory easy to count, stack, or transport. Folding in the flaps makes the box more durable too. I still can't stand unsecured flaps on a fully packed box!

I made a lot of friends at the hospital, and we hung out often. A crew of those coworkers became regulars at AUDIOBON shows. I was the same age as most techs and doctors, so they were a little more comfortable working with me. Extended lunch periods, passes for early dismissal, week-long parking lot privileges, meal compensations, and more were perks for veterinary assistants. Not being a pet owner allowed me to take on extra paid work for in home pet-sitting as well. Clients often inquired about pet sitting, which some Blum employees did on the side. (Blum did not provide those services).

Some other fond memories of Blum Animal Hospital include a lovely holiday party they held. Another time, a hospital vendor bought us rooftop seats across from Wrigley Field for a Cubs game. On yet another occasion, a group of us took a flying trapeze lesson. Blum was a giving and forgiving workplace, and if you didn't steal, show blatant disrespect, no-call/no-show, or abuse animals, you had a safe job.

The job itself was gratifying. One day, a doctor and I examined a seeing-eye dog brought in by its blind owner. The dog's owner said her trained yellow lab had been standing with its head against the wall and whimpering. I've always done my best to be sympathetic and helpful to people with blindness, which to me is one of life's most unfortunate disabilities. After a standard exam in the dog's mouth, the doctor noticed a foreign object lodged on a tooth. We held the dog's head, and he used medical-grade pliers to pull off the object. The plastic piece must have been stuck for a while because the smell that followed was putrid. This dog's immediate relief showed, and the owner was so grateful. It was a simple fix to what had been a big scare for her.

I had considered becoming a vet tech, but it entailed a lot of reading and science. Some assistants became techs and even went to vet school. I'd been there long enough to be seen as a rounded employee worth having. However, during traditional performance reviews that sometimes came with a raise and a list of acknowledgments, my employers raised concerns about my big-picture goals there. They didn't want assistants to remain assistants; they preferred to promote them to techs. I enjoyed the job, even the hospital scrubs (they were at least blue) but I wasn't a lifer anchored to one place with no ambition for anything else. I'd be a vet assistant there for ten years if I let them slide by!

Blum taught me about owning pets responsibly, knowledge that would pay off long-term. Loving an animal is not enough. Pet ownership requires time and money for emergencies and properly understanding the pet's individuality.

The experience helped further shape my life. I rescued a stressed out chinchilla from a client, whom I named Sméagol. While at the hospital, I had a lot of fun making goofy pages over the intercom and having non-work-related conversations. I learned that if a pet has teeth, it can and will bite: *Never* take the client's word that it won't bite.

I wasn't going to go any further in the business. I was now a veteran, and the only people there longer than me had moved up or remained stagnant as an assistant. My sister Teresa had left the VCC position and informed me of an opening where she was working.

I put in a two-week notice and received a lot of good wishes. On my last day, I thanked Dr. Rubin for having a practice that showed me an entire industry. I became a way more compassionate person towards pets, especially cats. I realized the automatic respect that comes with a "Doctor's" title. I like to joke that I'd get more respect if I wore a stethoscope. It's incredible how dismissive people are until the doctor walks in. Some people are sold on titles and will respect a fresh graduate over someone with ten years of experience. GET THAT FRAMED PAPER!

Chapter 39

Sunshine Home and Pet Care

Chicago, Las Vegas, Phoenix, 2003–Present
- Pet-sitter/free-loading house guest
- Total income unknown

Blum Animal Hospital often received calls for in-home pet-sitting, for which they did not provide. For me, it was a perfect chance to make extra cash. Those clients understood that Blum was not affiliated with employees' pet-sitting on their own time. I started my pet-sitting service, named after my mother's nickname for me: Sunshine.

I could take multiple pet-sitting jobs at once, and I still had my cell phone from JMA, which kept me connected and attentive to my clients. Not all pet-sitters were doing daily check-ins by cell phone in the early 2000s. I maintained a list of references and credentials for prospective new clients. Working at Blum satisfied most.

Cats were easy, usually a quick stop, Most cats tend to hide. Litter boxes and food bowls will tell you how the cat is doing.

Most dog owners wanted me to stay overnight at their homes. I didn't mind sleeping in their homes that were nicer than my apartment. It made it hard to return to my own home though. Once, the hot water at my apartment was out, and I didn't even know. My landlord was grateful I didn't complain; little did he know I hadn't been home all week.

I had a lot of wealthy clients whose pets were their only dependents. Many of my clients had horrible experiences with pet-sitters. The most common concern was a lack of communication. It's so simple: Just be reliable and keep your word. Once people trusted and relied on me, they became attached to using my service. It was nice to have different pets part-time.

My reasonable rates included collecting mail, watering plants, and handling service people visiting the home. I ensured clients weren't returning to a dirty home, especially the kitchen. The holidays kept me the busiest. Most clients were concerned whether I was comfortable. I became familiar with extensive TV setups and their various remotes. I had my own keys to multiple houses. Taking care of the pets was the easy part!

With so much entrusted to me, I deepened my respect of people's homes. I learned not to knock anything over. It's all expensive. I was working for myself, so I could wear blue jeans, workout attire, or even my pajamas!

Chapter 40

Classic Vending

Chicago, Illinois, 2005

- Driver/vending machine maintenance/junk food dealer
- Total income: $7,659.77

My sister Teresa had been working at Classic Vending, so she referred me for employment. Classic Vending had an office/warehouse in Chicago, twenty blocks west of my apartment. It was bikeable. If I had to take a bus, it was only one (no transfers). I was an inside referral, and my "interview" consisted of discussing the job and whether I wanted it. They had a lot of accounts and were a bit over their heads. However, in Chicago, there's no such thing as going over your head. You just hire more people to handle your growing business.

Classic Vending had white box trucks to deliver and maintain their various machines throughout Chicagoland. My route was up in the north suburbs, primarily schools with nice new vending machines. Maintenance and minor repairs on the vending machines were part of the job, for which I had no knowledge. Most repairs were done with assistance over the phone. Enter the cellular flip phone.

My day started with quickly loading the truck. We kept a lot of inventory in our trucks, but I always had to replenish sought-after products. Getting your truck loaded could be lengthy because other employees were trying to do the same. Plus, the shop was in a Chicago residential neighborhood, so we had to use an alley that might be blocked. Driving around in a truck wasn't always easy, either. Even though mine was a smaller box truck, some motorists had a special set of road behaviors reserved for truck drivers.

After arriving at an account, it was most efficient to visit every machine first to restock automatic inventory, collect money, and assess any needed repairs. Maximizing trips was essential, so I monitored the highest-selling products at every machine. This let me save time by bringing the top sellers with me on the way in from the truck.

People asking if a flower delivery is for them can be annoying, but they can be even worse when they see a cart full of snacks. Instead of "Are those for me?" the question became "Can I have one?" The amp volume was higher than when I worked at Mom's Early Learning Center (Chapter 1). They just aren't as cute as the kids at the day care center. It got ridiculous with teens swooping at me for handouts. If I was on the phone troubleshooting a machine, I'd be getting assailed by moochers. I started aiming my stops around lunches and after school dismissal.

It surprised me how many staff or other adults would interrupt my duties to discuss healthy eating. Classic Vending tried to put in nutritious snacks, but there's a massive problem with those: They don't sell! It's not a vending machine company's job to educate kids on healthy eating. They hired our service knowing what the machines would contain. The schools were so insistent on cutting out soda that we introduced Nestle Quik machines offering assorted flavors of milk. The irony was that flavored milk pumped the kids with just as much sugar as soda did.

The appearance of the vending machines was important, including having clean glass and no dust. The best machines had only dollar-bill feeds; collecting sliding mountains of coins was annoying. The newer machines were much less needy than older ones. They had digital readouts telling you what you needed without your having to count items or even open the machine. Another big part of the job was ensuring machines were closed correctly. If they were left open, people would accept the invitation to free goodies.

As I've alluded to, I've always liked working alone and being able to travel around. The best accounts were those without interruptions, such as offices, waiting rooms, and faculty lounges. The school routes would have been ideal for an evening position. Dealing with the students was simply too much. Whenever a vending-machine door swung open, it invited more than pleas for snacks: It attracted conversations from adults with nothing to do with their moments of free time. I didn't like making small talk while trying to take inventory—too distracting.

I prefer to be without distraction while counting money. There was never a shortage of people saying, "How about some for me?" as if thirty in singles was a pirate's payday. However, if I wanted to impress six-year-old nieces and nephews, I'd give them twenty singles instead of a $20 bill.

While I may seem to be giving ample air to the job's drawbacks, I liked working with my sister even though we rarely crossed paths. I had learned a lot about vending machine maintenance and gained yet more experience navigating the unpredictable Chicagoland roadways. Plus, I never went hungry!

After about six months, however, the work became an emptying balloon. The days were just too long. So, the hunt was on once again: I was back in job-search mode. Fortunately, I was offered a job, and I gave my two weeks' notice.

There'd been no need for professional delivery attire, and clothes weren't getting ruined. I could wear my blue jeans and be ready to go out after a long day at work.

Chapter 41

Aussie Mobile Pet

Oak Lawn, Illinois, 2005–06

- Mobile groomer/de-shed and shave-down technician
- Total income: $29,952.50

My friend Erika (co-worker at JMA, chapter 34) made departing Classic Vending a no-brainer when she called me one day. Her father, Bob, who lived in Oak Lawn, bought into a mobile grooming franchise called Aussie Mobile Pet and was looking for a groomer. I informed Erika that although I had experience handling pets for procedures, I was not qualified to groom them. She told me they would provide all equipment and train me. I said, "Yes!"

Most grooming jobs require having your own tools, but Bob had acquired it all. He purchased airfare, two weeks' worth of hotel accommodations, and rented a vehicle in Colorado for my training.

Colorado in April is snowy and cold but still sunny, a welcome stop on my general labor tour. I met at a well-run Denver franchisee's home office by 6 a.m. This required being in bed early the night before. Aussie Mobile Pet converted horse trailers into propane-

133

powered mobile grooming salons pulled by a mandatory white vehicle. Once powered, the trailer could run a shop vac, high-velocity dryer, clippers, air conditioner/heater, and water heater. A thirty-gallon water tank beneath the trailer supplied a full-sized tub. I was impressed with their organized fleet of mobile salons. Knowing all the trailer's ins and outs was necessary.

I trained with a nice girl who was efficient at her job. By then, MapQuest was in wide use, which allowed them to logistically route and schedule appointments.

Prep work for grooming is necessary. Overlooking even minor details can cost precious minutes. A five-minute delay for one appointment could often turn into a ten-minute delay for the next, and so forth. Appointments had to be completed inside two hours. My trainer was right on it. She had eight to ten appointments each day. By 7 p.m., she had the trailer cleaned and prepared for the next day. I was expected to learn trailer maintenance and how to perform basic haircuts. Breed cuts were not something learned in two weeks. Most appointments were simple shave-downs and de-shedding bathes. I felt confident with the job's customer service aspect and learned trailer maintenance quickly.

I learned to groom cats. Cats are completely different animals, and you must be extremely careful. Cat skin is very loose and can slice easily. Blade size #10 is considered safe, and that's it. Mobile grooming for cat owners is appealing because transporting is impossible for many cat owners.

They trained me to use a vacuum attachment to the hair clippers, a considerable advantage for all grooming. It keeps the blade cool, pulls the hair up, reduces arm stress, and saves cleanup time by vacuuming hair as it's cut. The vacuum system is a game changer for cat shave-downs. Cat hair can be relentless!

Although my trainer was compensated for my training, I gave her a gift card and a thank you note for having me shadow her that long. My two weeks in Colorado were good ones that prepared me to start working immediately upon my return to Illinois.

Bob bought a nice, new white pickup truck for me to pull the grooming trailer with. I could also use the truck for personal purposes such as hauling my drums. I felt a little weird because he was driving an old, used beater while I had the fresh ride.

In the beginning, we weren't that busy. I was guaranteed $50 a day, so I would typically start the day by picking up the trailer and then go wherever I could. Erika booked the appointments and contacted me throughout the day via two-way radio. They tried further growth through ads in sale papers and even a news spot on morning TV featuring me.

Their most responsive ads were the door hangers placed in the areas we wanted to work. Some prompted calls on the day of distribution. Putting up door hangers may sound easy, but it's not. It's a lot of walking up and down driveways. I started using a kick-scooter, and soon I could do fifty door hangers in thirty minutes. A major hurdle was finding a restroom. I started familiarizing myself with the local park reserves. I wondered how much it must have sucked for female mobile groomers to find a restroom.

They tried to keep my stops near my area, but it was tough. There weren't many mobile groomers then, so they took calls from all over. I don't know how I got away with some of those initial haircuts. Bringing the service to customers' homes was a big convenience for them and a huge advantage for us.

The internet was not yet an option for researching haircuts, so they sent me to the headquarters in California one weekend for an in-house course on breed cuts and clipping skills. Upon my completion of the course, we started taking the appointments I couldn't do before. Only a handful of standard dog breeds are vital to know, and those are enough to produce revenue. I could now look up the haircut in various grooming books and understand the patterns using specific blade sizes and comb attachments.

I never pre-shaved before that course either—a mistake. I thought I was saving wear and tear on the blades by clipping only clean, dry hair. I learned the blades could handle pre-shaving, and there was no reason to clean and dry a bunch of hair about to be clipped. Pre-shaving would have saved me so much time.

Mobile grooming had certain advantages over shops, such as finishing the appointment quickly. Some dogs cannot be around other dogs at a shop. Car rides for other pets were impossible. A pet's severe separation anxiety is the reason many owners seek out mobile groomers. Pet owners appreciate that they can be present during the groom. Customers often wanted a trailer tour, so we made sure it was always presentable. A fresh, clean smell went a long way. I always welcomed customers into my workspace.

Some grooming appointments involved only a nail trim. With a basic nail trim, the owners can assist if need be (insert light bulb idea balloon). Many owners appreciate not having to do nail trims; any who've tried understand.

While necessary, learning to drive a truck and trailer can be tricky. I practiced in large parking lots—once again, on my own. Blowing out all of that hair could be a project, so I preferred open space. Cleaning the trailer in an open lot would draw customers' interest without inviting complaints from grumpy neighbors.

I had many days where driving times were reaching high numbers. I conserved more money and time by bringing a cooler with food.

A lot of appointments had to be canceled because of difficult pets that had been turned away by other groomers. Gauging these challenges over the phone was tough, but that's the grooming business. You must weed through many new customers. Ideally, you will develop a base of steady clients that allows you to decline implacable customers or challenging pets. Until then, you stay patient as a groomer.

Taking appointments near where I lived wasn't an option, as I couldn't keep the trailer on a Chicago street overnight. The equipment would be stolen. There wouldn't be anywhere to park at a customer's house in the city.

Bob's territory was Tinley Park, about ten miles from his Oak Lawn home/office. I lived in Chicago. Complicating matters, Illinois had started a major freeway project that would cripple traffic for two years.

Aussie Mobile Pet started using diesel-run sprinter vans. This was preferable over a trailer! The vans had better gas mileage and were easier to keep cool or warm. They could run off the engine as opposed to a generator. After Bob bought one, he hired a woman who lived by him to take the appointments for that area.

I liked the job and could envision success with the right circumstances. But I had to acknowledge where I lived. We were too spread out in general and unable to grow in my immediate region. I could have been more successful if I'd lived in Oak Lawn or Tinley Park, but I wanted to stay in Chicago.

When I reached a year of employment, I had to be realistic. I considered Bob and Erika friends and didn't want to force their hand in letting me go. They were understanding when I gave my two weeks' notice. I felt terrible about having them invest in training, flights, hotels, and rental cars to develop and accommodate me. But Bob could now drive his truck, which I could tell he wanted to drive. I couldn't blame him. He was driving a clunker. I left on good terms with a reference, was still pet-sitting and—you guessed it—I had another job lined up.

I was grateful for my first job in a foreseeable trade, and I retain that knowledge to this day. While in the Denver airport after my two-week training, I started a list of all of my jobs. It appears in my table of contents.

Black pants/shorts were required with a black top. I discovered that scrub pants and a dry-fit shirt under a grooming smock worked best. They dried fast, didn't stain, and could be layered under to stay warm or rolled up to keep cool. I can tell you this, no way would I bathe pets, blow out hair, and try to move around in a trailer while wearing blue jeans!

Chapter 42

Fruit Flowers

Chicago, Illinois, 2006

- Delivery driver/lone wolf non-smoker
- Total income: $2,692.40

Fruit Flowers sold fruit cut into edible flower-shaped bouquets, and they opened a shop just blocks away from my apartment. Curiosity while riding home from the gym prompted me to apply in person. Upon my arrival, I was shown around the shop. It was run by spouses from New York with an accent to prove it. The wife was genuine and sweet and she loved dogs. She could tell by my questions I had delivery experience and hired me right away. It was a newly renovated shop, and I adapted there quickly.

Fruit Flowers was typically slow except on Saturdays. I was on call during the week. It was pull-time. They had branded, refrigerated delivery vans. The job wasn't complicated, and my working background prepared me. Fruit Flowers had been dealing with drivers just leaving arrangements wherever, such as on patios and in hallways. I would get deliveries into someone's refrigerator and return to the shop with an empty van and zero problems. Fruit Flowers wasn't used to that level of customer service. I thought that Fruit Flowers arrangements were a better gift than flowers. Cut-fruit bouquets were attractive, practical, tasty, and healthy. Delivery into human hands was not just necessary but instant advertising as well.

Because I was a non-smoker, they let me use the newest van. I kept it clean as a gesture of professional respect and consideration for others. Given my experience driving all over Chicago, I never needed a map or directions. I knew the city's street-grid system inside and out. You could drop me off anywhere blindfolded and I'd know by the address exactly where I was and needed to go.

Once again, having a clipboard, phone, bouquet, and uniform shirt got me buzzed into buildings. Deliveries were difficult to carry, and parking was frustrating. I inevitably started getting the same stupid question from strangers as I had at Ashland Addison (Chapter 37): "Are those for me?"

My workdays rarely went past 3 p.m., so I began working a door position at another bar for supplemental income. I would soon arrive at a defining moment, however. One day I came in and could hear the husband on the phone behind a closed door. He was yelling over and over at the top of his lungs at one of his employees: "Louis! Louis! You shut the f--- up, you shut the f--- up, Louis!" The bouquet designers working in the shop fled in terror, leaving just me and the wife. I am used to people losing their cool. It doesn't scare me, but it does concern me. The wife was embarrassed. It was hard for me to respect the husband after that. He'd shown his "Mr. Hyde." I decided I couldn't work for him. Plus, they needed to be busier.

Fruit Flowers helped me move on from Aussie Mobile Pet while adding to my experience with time management, vehicle maintenance, and Chicago deliveries. As long as I had the Fruit-Flowers polo shirt on, I was considered in uniform. My blue jeans weren't ripped, torn, or faded, so I still had one of my favorite perks. What can I say? You know me by now. Other peripheral benefits included being able to stop at my apartment for lunch while I waited for deliveries; meeting females on the job; and loading my mp3 player—not yet a simple task—from the shop's computer. Back to the general labor section I went. We were now in the age of internet job hunting. Enter craigslist.org.

Chapter 43

Underground Lounge

Chicago, Illinois, 2006–08

- Door guy/bar-back rat
- Total income: Not enough

Being single and childless, I always tried to have a second job. Underground Lounge was (and still is as of this writing) a Wrigleyville dive bar/live-music venue in the basement of a building. The entrance to the Lounge was at a disadvantage because it was a quarter- block off the Clark Street thoroughfare and its many bars.

Many bands including mine, AUDIOBON, played at Underground Lounge, which served as a hub for local starter bands and touring bands alike. It was a hip place with a personable staff. After AUDIOBON played one Saturday night, I talked to the bartender about a position for a "door guy." He had me come in on the following Monday to discuss it further and then return on Friday night to observe what the work and station would look like.

I became the Saturday-night door guy with an occasional Thursday-night shift. It paid $8 per hour plus two beers and sometimes an extra tip from the bartender. I could drink beer while working because I didn't abuse the privilege. I've always been a slow drinker.

It was a loose operation where the door guy charged a cover for the bands. The door guy kept track of who came and paid to see which band. Those bands got paid according to how many people they brought in. Most bands don't like the model because it's a catch-22: The band wants to play there to build a following, but the bar wants them to have a following to play there.

As I had at Lemmings, I tried my best to spot fake IDs, which isn't that simple. I received a complimentary book from the government that showed all the proper state IDs. If it's cold out, the lines are long, and you're transacting with cash, it gets a little crazy and you want to keep things moving. People can get impatient with showing ID. I still had to deal with the occasional "tough guys" who thought that door guys were fair game. I'd made it clear upon hiring that I wasn't touching anyone or breaking up fights, at least not by myself. In places like that, the bartender expects to handle fights, and there's no shortage of customer "heroes" ready to "save the day."

I did have to change the letters on the marquis, collect glasses, and sometimes change the keg. They wanted the door guy to remain upstairs at the door. I didn't mind staying at my post because the bar was a haven for smokers and radiator heat that can sizzle a sweat lodge! The main doorway led straight down to the basement bar, so I kept comfortable at the top of the stairs, which was more exciting anyway.

Wrigleyville is a bustling Chicago neighborhood, and I was back to being a fly on the wall. My time living in the city and working several jobs there had been sharpening my ability to assess and react to different situations. My experiences had taught me that a lot of people are quick to involve themselves in public dramas. I prefer to stand back, let it unfold, and watch the self-appointed heroes swoop in. There's an old adage that you shouldn't mess with people you don't know; they could be sicarios in chinos and cardigan sweaters. Interfering in street drama is a fool's errand.

At midnight, January 1, 2008, Illinois joined the rapidly growing movement to prohibit smoking in most public indoor places and workplaces. NO MORE CIGS! By now you can probably imagine my sense of rejuvenation toward nightlife. However, unfortunately for a door guy, it moved much of the smoke to right outside of the door. It was OK, though. I found it a small price to pay for smoke-free drinking and music gear that didn't wear ashtray body spray. Bar owners feared people would stop going to bars but didn't count on those like me who would now go out even more. The smokers wound up being more sociable with each other—out in the cold.

I now had instant radar for which women smoked. Before, it had sometimes taken me longer to detect because I'd be talking to a girl for a while, and then she'd break out the kryptonite by lighting a cig.

I didn't care for the guy in charge of Underground Lounge. He wasn't a musician. He would use the first $50 from the door cover charge to pay me. I thought, "Dis Guy!" He would call in to get revenue numbers and nitpick about the amounts received in relation to the number of people in the bar. I'd have to explain that band members didn't pay for their girlfriends.

If bands brought in a large following, they had a tough time tracking their turnout and so entrusted me with it. It was effortless for Dis Guy to misrepresent the turnout, which further spiked him on my chart of dislike. He wanted to pay the door guy and the sound guy with the band's gate money as opposed to his own. He demanded bands bring a following to ensure a "fair night's pay" for them and then fabricated the gate number. If he reported fewer people, he could pay us from the hidden margin.

For over a year, I had yet to move up. The bartenders were all former door guys. Things started going south once I realized I would never bartend. A door guy who'd started after me was given bartending shifts during the week, which meant I'd cover his Friday door shifts and an occasional Thursday shift. Dis Guy would hire females without experience while never offering me a chance to bartend. Dis Guy depended on me as a door guy because I was reliable and would sometimes do menial tasks. If I needed time off, I ensured coverage in advance. It was better than staying home.

After repeatedly being passed up to bartend, I stopped caring about working there. I reminded myself that I did not want to contribute to someone's drinking problem. Besides, AUDIOBON was playing out more, and I wanted the weekends off. I still had pull-time employment elsewhere, and ripping off the bands had taken its toll on me.

We had a mandatory staff meeting where I was told we had to work on New Year's Eve, which was not on a weekend or Thursday night. Until that moment, I hadn't been sure if I would be needed. I was miffed because I'd been looking forward to having New Year's Eve off, but I figured I could always use the extra money that Dis Guy said NYE would pay.

NYE was a super-busy night. I usually made $50, and that night, Dis Guy pitched in an extra $25 for me: a real Midas haul. It wasn't even close to being worth working on NYE. The bartender tipped me extra out of sympathy.

Eventually, I was working only Saturdays and ready to flash Dis Guy a double bird with the letters F and Y on separate fingers.

One night, he kept calling to get the counts, and I wasn't answering. At the night's end, I paid myself from the door as I was supposed to and decided to pay the bands fairly, providing an amount that likely exceeded Dis Guy's intent.

On the following Saturday night, he was calling in and demanding numbers again. I never took the calls and I paid the bands as I chose. What's he going to do from his couch? Dis Guy later questioned me about it in front of other staff. I told him straight up that I didn't steal from people and I wouldn't be ripping bands off for him anymore. Surprisingly, there was no consequence.

A few days later, I called Dis Guy and told him I wouldn't be coming in anymore. He never even asked why.

Oh well. Another steppingstone on the path to today. The job had been a profitable alternative to staying home on a Saturday night. I could see live music, talk to females, and go home with more money than I'd arrived with. With my faded blue jeans, I had been a fine fit within the business dress code.

Chapter 44

Peerless Imported Rugs

Chicago, Illinois, 2006–07

- Showroom grunt/champion of employee rights
- Total income: $19,525.00

I saw a general labor ad to apply in person for a "showroom assistant" position on what the platform of choice would now be for jobs, bands, cars, instruments, and whatever else the internet let out of pandora's box, craigslist.org. You could e-mail your resume as well. I emailed my résumé one evening outside of operating hours. I received a call the next morning from the showroom manager asking me to come in as soon as possible. It was an easy bike ride away.

Peerless Imported Rugs is a successful family-owned business founded in 1938. The owner was always on the move. Their personnel included installation, warehouse, sales, and office administration. They had an impressive showroom and a type of operation I was familiar with.

After a standard interview, I was hired as one of two showroom assistants, an entry-level position. The main function was to maintain the showroom and assist sales staff with the showing of area rugs and carpet samples. Even at the slowest of times, there was always dusting or vacuuming to do. We had a backpack shop vac for that duty. If you've seen the movie *Ghostbusters,* you already know the jokes and comments our equipment invited.

The facility was tucked into a typical Chicago building occupying its entire lot with three levels, multiple showrooms, and vast storage areas. Both the front and the back had several entryways, and the building made full use of its city-defining alleyway. They had a small tile showroom across the street that was part of another warehouse, which stored the tile inventory. I had to go to all of these locations daily for different tasks. Sometimes, it would be to assist a customer's pickup or unload a delivery from a truck.

The pay was $10 per hour, which was tracked with a traditional time clock and paper timecards. I worked every other Saturday with the preceding Wednesday off. Saturdays were retail—i.e., no contractors or deliveries—and so a lighter workday. I worked 10 a.m. to 6 p.m. daily if it didn't exceed forty hours (lunches were not paid). Many employers try to avoid paying overtime. I loved the schedule, which removed me from dealing with rush-hour traffic. Plus, because I took lunch from 2 p.m. to 3 p.m., I sidestepped the busy lunch crowds.

The job's leading challenge was assisting the sales staff and interior designers. As discussed in Carpetland USA (Chapter 23), interior designers are a significant part of this business. Many can be eccentric and, at times, difficult, but they represent repetitive business and substantial sales.

Rugs measuring 10' x 12' were stacked in piles throughout the showroom. They required two people to flip them so customers could see at least half of the rug. The fun part was when they wanted to see one laid out on the floor. On occasion, the store owner would pull a showroom assistant aside to reorganize the area rugs. It was the old "dig a hole and fill it back up" type of work. This seemed at times to be an act of frustration for him. On a whim, he would insist the piles weren't even enough, so he would have us restack them by placing the top rug on the floor next to the pile and then start restacking each rug.

The regular removal and re-hanging of rugs and straightening of the floor stacks was physically demanding. Other showroom-assistant responsibilities included menial work such as emptying trash and cleaning bathrooms. Nothing makes you question your job satisfaction like cleaning a bathroom. I was responsible for maintaining the entrances and walkways by sweeping them, removing debris, and, in winter, clearing snow and spreading salt.

The idea of being a showroom assistant was to somehow work your way up. If that didn't happen, you might be treading water there for years.

Finding distractions from the job's boredom-inducing monotony became requisite too. Anything I could do to get out of the store while still on the clock was a plus. I would surf the web and texting was becoming more common and not yet frowned upon while at work.

I did like this job. The hours never interfered with my music. I could ride my bike to work. Nice-looking women often came into the showroom. I could arrive to work tired or even hungover.

As I approached a year of employment, I started to consider my future. Seeing me as resourceful, committed, and reliable, coworkers began wondering why I was still an assistant. Unfortunately, this was another job for smokers. Almost the entire staff smoked, even the owner. If I was asked to assist in the warehouse/smoker's lounge, I stated and acted on my right to occupy a space that was smoke-free while I was in it.

One day, the owner went off on us in a bout of managerial dyspepsia because there was no one to help him while I cut carpet in the warehouse. A handful of others were smoking when he entered the warehouse and claimed he could replace us quickly, and there was no shortage of slackers to give jobs to. I remember thinking there was no shortage of employers looking for good employees.

Once again, my winding professional road was rolling straight at a fork. So far, segments of my career path, if that's what you want to call it, were still random rocks gathered by my transient destiny's hand. A familiar feeling had returned for its job-related refrain: I no longer wanted to work there.

I started searching for a new job on one of the showroom computers. I had a laptop at home that could connect to a weak and unsecured signal nearby to search Craigslist for general labor ads. I would then bring my resume on a flash drive to the terminal at work the next day. I even used the company fax machine for my hunt.

Now for the positive takeaway. I saw a new world of rugs I had not in previous showroom-assistant positions. One can make a living selling high-end area rugs, and Peerless's showroom was extensive. People really will pay top dollar for what lies on the floor.

Finding another job was a cinch. I gave a two-week notice, and because I left on good terms, I had additional experience for my résumé, as well as a favorable reference in the sales manager.

With easy work that wouldn't ruin them, the job had been perfect for blue jeans. I could head straight out after work to the neighborhood bars. I didn't want to buy other work pants. In hindsight, I might opine that navy-blue work pants might have offered greater flexibility, but as usual I followed my modus operandi to wear what I wanted whenever I could.

Chapter 45

Relax the Back

Chicago, Illinois, 2007

- Very patient delivery driver/recipient of verbal Nerf balls
- Total income: $6,584.16

The General Labor section on craigslist.org had an ad for a delivery driver at an ergonomic furniture shop called Relax the Back. The location was a few miles from my apartment. I could bike it. My résumé prompted a quick response.

Two sisters owned this location. Sister 1 did all the admin and accounting work from home. Sister 2 ran the day-to-day operations at the shop. My interview was simple. All I had to do was bring my valid, violation free driver's license, dress casually, and reassure them I could do the job described.

Sister 1 explained in my interview that I was hired as the primary delivery driver. A younger guy was currently doing the job, but reliability had become an issue. They trusted his ability to do most of the work, but they didn't want him managing. Plus, the job included a lot of direct interaction and contact with customers. He didn't shave, reeked of cigarettes, always wore the same clothes, and looked like he'd just rolled out of bed. The business needed a higher level of representation.

We delivered ergonomic desk chairs that improved one's posture and comfort to various Chicago offices. The chairs were pricey but worth it. After delivering the chair, I would align the customer in it properly at their desk. I removed the old chair, which neither the customer nor the store would want. I would put it in the truck, take it home, and resell it!

For the first two weeks, I observed the other driver, aiming to go with the flow without making waves. As a Chicago delivery guy, I would again need to be familiar with the delivery entrances for the city's significant buildings downtown. I quickly learned how to assemble chairs with speed and precision. As I did, I noticed the current guy's assemblies were missing small parts that I deemed necessary. If the manufacturer spent money to include them, they were essential, I believed.

I handled deliveries and managed inventory Monday through Friday from 9 a.m. to 5 p.m. No Saturdays! Driving a large delivery truck around Chicago on a Saturday was too great a liability. Relax the Back avoided overtime at all costs. My job further included maintaining the showroom by vacuuming, dusting, cleaning glass, restocking, and emptying trash cans—again with the damn coffee grinds and drippings [see Chapter 13]. Ugh.

At the end of my two-week shadow period, the current guy messed up good. He already drove like a maniac, but this time he was tailgating someone and rear-ended them. I drove us back to the shop and on the way explained why I'd been hired. It was simply the right moment to let him know I would now be his boss. With the damage to our vehicle riding in front of us, I didn't have to get into much deeper detail.

He knew this meant he'd be working fewer hours than me, as in being the first sent home on slower days. After that, I could tell he wouldn't do anything more than he was asked. He understood the job; he just didn't understand being professional. A delivery driver is the company's face to the public. However, there was still plenty of work for him to do.

It didn't take long to identify that Sister 2 was a problem. She was a bona fide micromanager, and many of us know how easy those people are to please. She constantly called my cell asking about drop-off times while I was out delivering. She didn't account for traffic or parking in her expectations and scheduling. She second-guessed everything from cycle counts to where and when something was placed. I organized the basement disarray of storage to reflect the order of the cycle-count sheet. Sister 2 did not appreciate the new arrangement. Rather, she addressed it as a waste of time because "it won't stay that way."

It got so bad that during one delivery, the customer said he recognized me from a few days before when Sister 2 was going off on me in the showroom. Shortly after that very day, Sister 2 confronted me from inches away and accused me of improperly taking inventory. I can still feel the specks from her speech. I backed up and said, "Hey, what's with spitting in my face?" I pointed out that the sign-off in question didn't remotely resemble my signature. She stormed off, sat at her desk in another room, and continued yelling at me. Everyone in the store could hear her, and they gave me a "whoa" look.

I released a big sigh of relief and gathered my belongings. One of the salespeople saw the ease on my smiling face and asked, "You're walking out of here, aren't you?" I went to Sister 2's office and let her know she wouldn't have to worry about me anymore. She tried to stop me from leaving, but I walked out, got on my bike, and rode home.

I was already job searching, but this episode put the kibosh even on providing a two-week notice. I made side cash playing music, pet-sitting, and selling used chairs. I'd be OK for a while.

The main positives: I learned to ace furniture setups and assemblies, and I did appreciate and benefit from personal use of the truck.

It can often be disappointing when a blue-jeans job doesn't work out. Assembling and delivering these chairs was easy on the wardrobe. I liked that I didn't have to sport a company uniform and could wear what I wanted if I didn't exhibit rips, tears, holes, or logos.

Chapter 46

Pet & Plant Care Service

Chicago, Illinois, 2007

- Pet-care resource/dog-poop suspect
- Total income unknown

Walking off my job at Relax the Back wasn't ideal, and I needed to find something. My lifelong friend Lefty recommended me to Pet & Plant Care Service. I stopped into their Lincoln park office to fill out an application and was hired after a quick interview.

I had my own vehicle, but I preferred to bike it, which was doable though not always favorable due to weather or last-minute requests that might require greater trips to accommodate. The work was easy, but unfortunately, it didn't keep me busy, and I worked just a few days a week. As at many of these services, the turnover rate was high.

Dog walking is cool. You can make good money, set your hours, and meet great pets. On the downside, it's not steady, and a lot of people, mainly neighbors, blame dog walkers for any nearby poop on the ground when they should be barking at the pet owners. I did not like the margin left for the worker from what the service charged. The pay just wasn't worth working for somebody else; I would have been far better off with my own dog-walking service.

When winter approached, I realized I didn't want to walk dogs in the cold. I didn't quit or get fired. Rather, I dropped off all the keys assigned for one week and stopped calling in. They stopped calling back. It was mutual and effortless.

Back to the drawing board I went on my multi-stop tour of general labor jobs. One of the nice things about dog walking was that there wasn't any real dress code. Few people saw me, and if they did, I was an afterthought. No blue-jean restrictions here, I suppose I could even have tears, rips, or holes. Who was going to complain—the dog?

Chapter 47

Elizabeth Arden
Red Door Spa

Chicago, Illinois, 2007–10
- Inventory management/schmoozer
- Total income: $39,502.39

Craigslist's General Labor section advertised an assistant to the retail business manager (RBM) at Red Door Spa on Michigan Avenue. I'd had my own manicures a few times before, but that was it. This would be a foreign work environment.

Red Door Spa was on the ninth floor of the 909 building on Michigan Avenue. Red Door Spa and Elizabeth Arden were founded in 1910 on New York's famous Fifth Avenue. New York was the flagship location, but Chicago was just as busy. The position I was applying for was offered only at these two locations.

This was retail, so proper dress was necessary. I prettied my résumé without exaggeration. The cons of overstating one's job history are obvious. Mine featured employable assets such as customer service, facility maintenance, inventory management, reliability, valid driver's license, and reliable transportation. I emailed my résumé and received a call for an interview with the retail business manager (RBM), and it was more of a tour. I was hired. The spa consisted of estheticians, massage therapists, hair stylists, manicurists, and receptionists. I was welcomed right away. There were several managers, so I had to tread lightly with my humor. I was successful at it for a while.

It paid $10 an hour, but it was an excellent job. I rode my bike and worked a flexible schedule, so if I did drive, parking on meters at night was usually a non-factor.

At first, it was all about whatever the RBM wanted me to do. The RBM was responsible for receiving Chicago's rather large deliveries of products and tracking inventory, so she was allowed an assistant. The trick for them was justifying keeping me at thirty-two hours or under a week to avoid making me eligible for insurance. Pull-time!

There was a high turnover rate with the retail/admin staff, many of whom could be friendly but snide. I managed to stay out of it all. People often commented that I got along with everyone. Drama in a place such as this is innately baked in; avoiding it is as simple as steering around a boulder in the road. We can often fare better with our coworkers by aiming to be pleasant and polite but properly distant from personal land mines.

The RBM quit Red Door a year into my employment, freeing up a massive part of the payroll. I was doing the functions of that job, so management saved an entire salary.

Salon management determined their best strategy would be to have me maintain an RBM's inventory duties without an RBM's pay. I was not going to sell make-up or manage front staff cats. I certainly didn't meet corporate qualifications for the RBM position. I wouldn't make more than $10 per hour. For some people, that might have been a deal breaker. Management could, however, offer job security, salon services, and justifying my paycheck to corporate. In a good spirit, I added a condition of my own to my role: I would have open access to any food brought in by clients. Management and department heads were a-okay with that. To an extent, I already had been helping myself. In other words, I changed my status from an unofficial moocher to an official one.

The corporate office sent us schematics for retail displays. Regional managers would visit and perform a walk-through to ensure ours matched the schematics. If they did, the regional managers would be happy; hence, our manager was happy. Considering the importance of complying with corporate requests, I would get tweaked when the admin staff rearranged my displays, which presented each product in the order listed on the supply sheets. Other staff members attributed their rearranging of the displays to being bored or having OCD. I repeatedly explained that regional managers didn't care how "you" wanted it to look. OCD and boredom weren't legit reasons to screw with another person's proper work!

All retail merchandise was monitored and tallied through a system called SAP requiring a log-in to their server. The proper retail inventory arrived once I began to do cycle counts correctly and on time. This was a benefit to employees trying to collect commissions by selling products. Training others on SAP was difficult. Sometimes, I came in just for a retail cycle count.

Properly labeling and pricing items made for quick counts and eliminated waiting for an employee's attention for a simple price check. This way, they could "clerk" the apparent stuff—i.e., ring up something someone already wants to buy. With good product knowledge, you might start inquiring further about commissions for selling a product. In other instances, if a brand representative came in to educate staff about a product and you were already informed, a professional door could open for you.

Each department head had been responsible for counting its own supplies. The RBM had never collected counts and automatically ordered five to ten of everything once a month for a year. We had an excess inventory with miniscule storage. I managed to get return authorizations on three different shipments, resulting in $10,000 in spa credit!

I then organized each department's supply stock on its own shelving unit in the order of the supply sheets. With this system, counting and re-ordering inventory took less than ten minutes. Just as important, my count sheets allowed the department heads to stay within their budgets. l could know if the slightest item was missing or moved. The supply warehouse for the entire chain was in Illinois, so the manager would sometimes have me take her SUV to pick up supplies (my valid driver's license in action proving its value).

I had complete control over the supplies as well as keys to the entire spa. I knew when the shipments were arriving, so I could do all receiving, stocking, and label-printing after-hours. No Saturdays dude!

Red Door invested in a remodel. Construction lasted about six months, requiring us to move the retail supplies and displays, cover areas with plastic, and clean up the dust. Management knew I would be reliable for this kind of stuff. They depended on me entirely for deliveries, supplies, facility maintenance, and more.

After the remodel, management was pressured to get an RBM. They interviewed potential RBMs here and there when someone on high inquired about it, but they never filled the position, which solidified my job until I wanted to go.

I enjoyed working at Red Door Spa. I could even store in the onsite stock room my work uniform, which consisted of pants, a polo shirt, and shoes—all black. Red Door provided the polo shirts; I found black pants at the thrift store. I would change into the uniform when I arrived, and the housekeeping department would launder my other work clothes. After-hours counting inventory or unpacking supplies were blue-jean opportunities, still preserving a chill atmosphere with cool people for me to make friends with.

One of them was a hair stylist named Laura. Laura was the spa's busiest hair stylist. Being married to a musician, she loved going to see live bands. We shared a good vibe as well as things in common. Laura is a hip woman, and she became an LLF of mine. When it came time to finally cut my shoulder-length hair, she fit me into her packed schedule to perform the honors. Her clients became her friends, which is the best way to build your client base.

When a unique opportunity to move back to the Southwest arose, I gave Red Door Salon more than a two-week notice. There was no need to worry that they'd terminate me early, which could often be a risk elsewhere. I tried to train potential replacements how to do what I did, but filling my black work shoes would require some effort. By that point I'd become tough to replace. The department heads knew they'd have to do their own inventory and were bummed.

It was a smooth departure. The whole staff was great about saying goodbye and wishing me luck. They even brought in a big cake, collected signatures, and put money in a farewell card. A part of me felt proudly appreciated for the value I'd be leaving behind.

Working throughout Chicago had continued forging me into the working adult I was and still am. I was leaving Red Door Spa with three years of experience including inventory management, retail sales, special orders, facility maintenance, and self-management. For what would be my last job in the city, working on Michigan Avenue amongst great people was an excellent time.

Now thirty-five, I would go back on the general labor tour across the country. I was happy to leave Chicago on good terms. I almost cried—almost.

Chapter 48

Streetside Bar and Grill

Chicago, Illinois, 2008
- Door dude/smoking-enforcement Terminator
- Total income unknown

While working pull-time hours at Red Door Spa, I saw a general labor ad on craigslist.org for a door guy at a neighborhood bar called Streetside Bar and Grill on Armitage Avenue. I sent a relevant résumé and was called in for a quick and easy interview. They wanted someone for Saturday nights and offered $50, a food order, and a beer at the end of the shift. AUDIOBON had a lot of Friday-night gigs, so working Saturday nights would work out.

I trained with the door guy who was moving to bartending. It was an effortless operation. They had a small kitchen that closed by midnight with outside seating, and it was my duty to stack the outside chairs and cable- lock them to the tables at night's end.

If there ever was trouble, I could rely on the bartender or fellow patrons to help. I only ever had to ask a few drunkards to leave, and if they didn't comply, calling the police was the protocol. There were times when troublemakers didn't care about the prospect of cop intervention. At that point, they entered the next stage: public humiliation, a polished technique I gladly applied. It typically involved the indignity of informing the bartender right in front of them that they could not drink anymore and then letting their peers know that their fellow patron had to leave.

Door duty entailed babysitting smokers as well. I say babysitting because of how adolescent smokers can be about their habit. Smoking was supposed to be at least fifteen feet away from the entrance. Many smokers moved that boundary to right in front of the door, congesting the entrance to the bar. They would open the door for people, a gesture that came with inhaling their secondhand smoke. It wasn't a fair trade. I imagined that, like me, many customers would rather have opened the door themselves than breathe the smoke.

Smoking in the outside dining area was prohibited. However, many smokers thought that lighting up outside removed the secondhand-smoke factor. I'd often have to ask people not to smoke in the dining area, which prompted some to throw a fit. They would "comply" by holding their cigarette over the top rail. I'd have to remind these individuals that wasn't cutting it. With the Smoke-Free Illinois Act of 2008 now in effect, I usually received gratitude from other diners.

By then, I'd accepted that I was never going to bartend. It just wasn't me. I liked the job and did it for a year, including a winter season and the extra dynamic it adds laying salt and clearing walkways. It was extra cash earned on a Saturday night while not spending money. It also featured meeting females.

One night, there was a traffic accident in front of the bar. It didn't faze me too much. Someone tried to beat the red light at the busy intersection and rear-ended a car stopped in traffic. It looked worse than it was. The people were out of the cars and talking, but the bartender was yelling at me to go out and check on them. I looked out the window and said, "They're fine." I guess traffic patrol had been added to my door-guy position, because he continued insisting that I go outside and investigate. I said, "No, that's not my job."

After that episode, a lower-energy establishment vibe developed, wrapping itself around my declining enthusiasm. It was what it was: a short-term part-time gig I could list on my résumé. I gave my notice. Pull-time at Red Door would suffice.

Streetside was a casual environment that would have allowed even faded blue jeans for working. My main issue was I didn't think mine were tight enough: Skinny jeans seemed to be the *mode du jour* there.

Chapter 49

Mother's Nightclub

Chicago, Illinois, 2009
- Percussionist
- Total income unknown

The Original Mother's is a nightclub famously featured in the movie *About Last Night*. The downstairs had a large rectangular bar in the center and a dance floor that ran against a long, mirrored back wall which featured a percussionist playing with the music.

As a percussionist, I was invited to attend one of their mandatory Thursday promo staff meetings. Being on time mattered. I was still employed at Red Door Spa, which was a couple blocks' walk away, so all I had to do was work a little bit later on Thursdays. Mother's hired young female emcees to encourage the crowds to dance and socialize. Most emcees were models and actors. I sat through the Thursday meeting noting there were a lot of girls and only two drummers, which was *bueno*.

After the meeting was dismissed, I auditioned to an empty room save for the main manager playing music from the DJ booth. Mother's had their own percussion setup, which made things simple. I played along with one song and returned the following Thursday to be introduced as the new Saturday-night drummer. Another drummer—an admirable player—performed on Friday nights. I went in on several Fridays to observe him.

Playing percussion would be a better use of my time than door duty. I would play drums, drink for free, and get paid. Moderate drinking for emcees and drummers would be comped by Mother's as well.

Getting a nap in before my shift was always a good idea, because it was a long night coasting through Top 40 and 80s pop songs. Playing this gig from 10 p.m. to 4 a.m. on Saturdays paid my rent! It refined my sense of timekeeping and live presence. Mother's is in a part of town with a bulls-eye for tourists. The music was predictably status quo for partying. The playlists could be tough at times. In my view, certain genres didn't line up well with live percussion; for me, hip-hop was one. When they started playing blocks of hip-hop and rap, I would take breaks.

I brought my own percussion pieces to complete the drum setup. I can tell you this: The cowbell always draws crowds. I included two cowbells in my setup: one for me and one pointed outward for patrons to play as part of the fun. I could even come out from behind the kit and work the floor with the crowd.

I *never* let bar customers play the drums. Some would interrupt me while playing to ask if they could get on my kit. First, you don't interrupt someone who's playing live, period. Second, I don't know you. How do I know you can play? Because you say so? Nah. Third, if you do play, and you're good, you typically aren't so desperate to go that you'll risk making another drummer look bad. Fourth, I had to audition to an empty room on a weekday to get the gig, so the station is earned.

The only thing worse than the direct interruptions were the guys who sent their girlfriends to ask. I'd be in the middle of playing, and a girl would walk up smiling and batting her eyes. She'd be saying something. While playing I would lighten up and ask, "What's up?" She would reply, "Can my boyfriend play your drums?" I just responded with a simple "no" and kept playing.

This gig further refined my increasingly serious perspective about music as a pursuit. Playing gigs that didn't pay in non-desirable situations and locations was fading farther into my rearview. To be gainful, I had to never take paying opportunities for granted. Unless my bands were getting paid the same or better for a show booked far enough in advance for me to get a Mother's shift covered, I wasn't taking a Saturday night off. I never canceled, called in, or no-showed. I was always on time, and I played with energy until the last call for alcohol.

Overall, the gig lasted for about a year, and I did enjoy it. Looking back on it at the end, I recognized some things I would have done differently performance-wise. If I found a gig like Mother's again, I would coordinate more with the DJ rather than play in a musical lane that was tuned-in and present but separate.

Club attire was required for patrons, who would be denied entrance if wearing jeans or non-collared shirts. As the club drummer, I was exempted from this policy. I wore my nice jeans without rips, holes, tears, or fringe. I liked that I was performing in a club, so I even observed the collared-shirt requirement.

I loved the life I had built over fifteen years of living in an excellent location. My neighborhood had changed from sketchy and dangerous to artsy and cool, and finally, condominiums and baby strollers. I packed up my drums one last time ready to leave my beloved Chicago and take them on my general labor tour out west.

Chapter 50

Trent Seigler

Henderson, Nevada, 2010–11

- Childcare/funcle
- Total income: Free room and board

This chapter is personal, and I've tried to share it objectively, just stating the facts that relate to the work. I got the job by word of mouth (on the marble).

A Chicago friend once asked me what I thought about being a caretaker for her four-month-old daughter. She didn't trust daycare. When I told my sister Teresa about this offer, she countered with free room and board in a winter-free climate where she was now residing in Nevada. My nephew Trent was only a couple of months old, and it was time for his mom, Teresa's partner Jen, to return to work. I had first met Trent at my brother Fred's house when Teresa and Jen brought Trent to Chicago to meet family. Trent had just learned to get on his hands and knees and was teething. He kept gumming on the smooth, cool marble tiles in front of the fireplace. I pretended to do the same; we've been buddies ever since.

My mother had moved to Nevada a few years earlier and was thrilled that I was even thinking about moving there. In November 2010, I moved out west. Leaving cold and wet weather!

Teresa had a college student's schedule, and I would care for Trent during Jen's banker's hours—yes! This was by far the easiest job I've ever had. My commute to work was a dream: I woke up and walked downstairs.

I knew that this "job" was temporary. Childcare is that way. Kids grow up and go to school. With that being the case, I job-searched at my leisure. It would be a while before I could take a full-time job. Trent was still a baby in diapers. They were not hurrying to put him in any daycare. Trent was such a good baby; I loved spending time with him. He was personable and not shy at all. Those first months were precious, and I was glad to be a part of them.

Nap time became something I learned to appreciate. Feeling he might miss something otherwise, Trent rarely slept more than thirty minutes. He invented the "pinky nail technique": poking his eye to tears to fight falling asleep. I had never seen a baby fight sleep like him. Once he was finally under, I had to slowly crawl out of his room. Nylon pants were out of the question, because that little bald head would pop up if you made one tiny brushing sound on the floor. For some reason, landscapers loved using leaf blowers outside his window during nap time.

It's necessary to be a trustworthy caretaker for someone's child. Although it is easy, it is a huge responsibility. Trent may have been a "job" but he was always my nephew. I love that kid. His existence changed my life. I have so many memories of those days with that little guy!

After nine months, Jen and Teresa started using a daycare to get Trent used to being around others. Teresa had graduated and now had more time. I still cared for Trent a few days a week, but I could focus more on looking for work. I started with a search for something at least part-time. I could show reliability, and Jen was always willing to be a reference. It helps to have family members as references without the same last name as yours.

This was a legitimate work relationship worthy of adding to my résumé. Along with room and board, Jen would still pay me cash here and there. She always treated me fairly. It is much easier if families who work together keep the work aspect in mind. We've had a great working relationship for years.

It was a valid gap in my employment. Many west-coast employers are worried that you're a snowbird who will flee as soon as the heat arrives. Having a solid foundation in Nevada was reassuring for potential employers.

This was my first experience working from home. I was most likely to sleep and work in my basketball shorts and lightweight sleeveless shirt. Considering my customer was wearing a diaper, I'd say I was presentable. Jen and Teresa had been planning a move to Phoenix. I would soon have to find a place to live and a paying job!

Chapter 51

C1 Staffing

Las Vegas, Nevada, 2011
- Manual laborer/standard stock grunt
- Total income: $185.00

When I moved to Nevada, I promptly acquired a state-issued driver's license. Las Vegas is such a transient city that having a local ID made a difference. It initiated greater leniency in the event of a police pull-over. It often doubled as a free-entry pass into almost any Las Vegas nightclub.

While living with Jen and Teresa, I saw a Craigslist ad in General Labor for setting up special events with a staffing agency called C1. I had state proof I was local, reliable transportation, and proper attire.

After a very quick and basic group interview I was hired. I worked a few nights when they needed mass staffing. These were minimum-wage jobs setting up and breaking down tables and chairs in large convention rooms. January and February are busy with conventions in Las Vegas.

All I did was stand in a line and push stuff on wheels. I always use work gloves, a box cutter/knife, a winter hat, layered pants, and neckwear. Work gloves are great for moving furniture, as are steel-toed black shoes. I would never do work like that again without steel-toed shoes.

I dressed warmly because on the job you might be waiting outside for a while, sometimes early in the morning or later at night. It may have been Nevada, but it was still wintertime. It can get chilly. Those loading docks were wide-open spaces, and the winds were strong.

There is never a shortage of know-it-alls on these jobs, but it's easy work if you stick to your "temp" role. Being on time, staying late, and following instructions increased chances for a callback.

This addition to my résumé showed that I was still looking for work even though my priority was daycare for my nephew Trent. It was nice to get out of the house, make some extra cash, and be social.

Chapter 52

Divine Entertainment

Las Vegas, Nevada, 2011

- Character actor/mascot
- Total income: $180.00

The entertainment section of craiglist.org is often flooded with adult ads, but you can filter those out. Venturing outside my trusted general labor section I saw an ad seeking actors to play mascots.

Divine Events hired actors to attend events in costume. Applying was simple. I provided head shots, an entertainment résumé, and a local ID. My interview was brief, and I started the following weekend.

Divine Events had me attend a Monster Truck Rally as a mascot. I wasn't sure what to expect. I met the point person who guided me and three other actors to a designated tent and assigned us each a mascot character. The characters represented a few popular drivers at this Monster Truck Rally. Mine was modeled after a Hispanic driver named El Toro Loco. The costume was a bright-orange shirt sporting an oversized bull's-head mask. Each of us was assigned a handler to guide us through the crowds. Helpful! It wasn't easy to see in those costumes.

They had us attend Monster Truck events all weekend, including a dance contest and lots of picture-taking. It was easy money and provided a meal. I capitalized on the anonymity. You can be as animated as you want in a disguise like that.

The two-day gig was the only job I ever got with Divine Events. Many of their bookings were for birthday parties I didn't want. Overall, it was fun, and I was able to add photos to my entertainment résumé. I could wear blue jeans, and I did on the first day. On the second day, the orange mascot shirt and bull's-head mask went better with black cargo pants, black canvas high-top shoes, and black drumming gloves.

Chapter 53

Book It Las Vegas

Las Vegas, Nevada, 2011
- Attempted actor (again)
- Total income unknown

I was successful with one Craigslist ad in the entertainment section, which was rare, but it was Vegas. I saw one for background extras of all kinds. Book It Las Vegas was a small entertainment company. I went into the office on the first day they placed the ad.

They staffed birthday parties, which I wasn't interested in. Book It hired me only once for a casino background scene shot late one night with no speaking lines. I stood there, laughing at the roulette table, pretending to be enjoying myself. Easy.

It was another situation where I felt irrelevant to the overall scenario. Eat last, don't ask questions, and be grateful for the seventy-five bucks you'll get in a few weeks. I know acting careers often have rough beginnings, but I had no desire to live like that for long. Extras must be available on any day, making a regular job nearly impossible.

I'd get my performing fix instead with what I loved most: my drums. I got a few more calls from Book It, and after I kept turning them down, they quit calling. Birthday parties as Barney? No way man!

The dark blue jeans I wore were acceptable requisite club attire for the one gig I did.

Chapter 54

Las Vegas Parking

Las Vegas, Nevada, 2011–13

- Parking lot attendant/valet/choont
- Total income: $2,178.64

I saw an ol' Craigslist ad in general labor for temporary parking lot attendants that included details about large group interviews.

Las Vegas Parking was family-owned and like the operations I saw in Illinois. They held a mass hiring to cover an annual March weekend at the Las Vegas Motor Speedway. This was another scenario where being properly dressed was important. March in Nevada is beautiful during the day. Being outside was pure sun exposure, and headwear was the only real UV protection. It cools down at night, and having a knit hat, neckwear, and gloves was essential. I wore thermal pants.

My first assignment as a lot attendant was to wave people into spots in assembly-line fashion at the speedway. There were a lot of pick-up trucks!

Many people parking in lots tend to be rude to those working the lot. One driver who was repeatedly dropping individuals off at the front entrance got particularly annoyed when we directed him where to park. He would yell, "Dropping awfff!" For the rest of the night, whenever someone was just dropping off, all of us working the lot would holler, "DROPPIN' AWFFF!", including when the annoyed guy returned. It was fun.

A lot of attendants inquired about valet jobs. They would ask one another and anyone who seemed in charge about any possible openings among the many valet accounts. If you could become introduced to a valet manager overseeing the speedway event, you might finagle a valet shift. You just had to follow the basic event mass-hiring rules: Show up on time in uniform (all black) and compliantly follow instructions.

Las Vegas Parking had accounts throughout the valley. Even though the large casinos had their own valet service for the main entrances, they hired small companies to handle retail entrances. I trained at a retail entrance at one of the large casinos. The loading zones were completely covered with large spaces and a parking lot right around the corner from the valet stand. The whole front area including the stand was fully shaded all year from the sun. I asked one of the guys how to get a shift there, and he said someone must die!

I spent a few months filling shifts throughout Vegas for special events. Many of the valets couldn't operate a stick shift, which pointed calls my way. Las Vegas Parking ran parking for the annual Las Vegas Market furniture show at the World Market Center. This was the first time I got to be a golf-cart driver. That's the kind of job people do for fun. After a day of my golf-cart driving, management saw the tips I reeled in and kept me in the cart for the event's remainder.

I started working a regular graveyard shift at a forty-floor high-rise just west of the strip. The building offered complimentary valet and even had a valet office where I could hang out (and sleep in). Las Vegas Parking struggled to keep the shift full because the property managers wanted the same person each night. Filling the daytime and even the second shift was no problem. They had issues only with the graveyard shift.

It was worth it most of the time. There were always scavs who didn't live there and used the complimentary valet service without tipping. That went with the territory.

I got a call to fill a different graveyard shift at a boutique motel. I wasn't exactly sure what made it boutique, other than that perhaps it welcomed an array of lifestyles. The motel fashioned itself as a type of late-night destination for the party-hard populace.

It was a super easy gig close to where I was living. The shift would be from 11 p.m. to 7 a.m. In getting started, I was supposed to meet up with a fellow valet who regularly worked there, a younger, married white guy named Tyrell. I mention white only because beforehand I knew just his name, and I made certain assumptions about who I'd be meeting. Once Tyrell and I became familiar with each other, we started referring to certain people as "choonts." We'd picked it up from overhearing a Mexican in the kitchen staff who used the word for different numbskulls whose behaviors might come into view on congested, busy nights. We would say, "What's with this choont?" I still say it.

There was a lot of partying at this motel, as well as many choonts who wanted to use the complimentary valet but were not motel guests for whom the service was intended. Often when the motel guests had parties, some of their party choonts felt they could use the free service too.

My last shift at this account involved a super-choont. When we refused service because he wasn't a guest, he tried to pull rank by parking in the drive to obstruct business. I ignored him, which only peeved him more. I even asked his girlfriend if she was really dating this choont.

Las Vegas Parking provided a laid-back, yet professional image of standard black shorts or pants and their white branded polo shirt. Las Vegas Parking could only offer a few graveyard shifts. It was a simple, good, and occasional part-time job. I didn't want to start valet parking full-time again. It's tough on the body. I never had a problem with any of the people running this company. I hope they are still going strong.

Chapter 55

Deal Time Las Vegas

Henderson, Nevada, 2011

- Production assistant/viper
- Total income: $3,963.12

Trent was in daycare half the week, so I could apply for a pull-time job. After a few stints with temp agencies and few calls to valet park, I checked the General Help section of craigslist.org to find an ad requesting retail/warehouse help right down the road. The business, Deal Time Las Vegas, was owned by a married couple. They bought wholesale goods and resold them on a local televised auction.

I stopped in and met the husband. He was wearing jeans and a t-shirt and sporting a bed-head. Seeing I was armed with a résumé he could tell I was job hunting and started with the basic questions. I was available to start immediately, and he concluded a two-minute interview by offering a job that would pay me $10 per hour.

It was a giant square facility with a showroom for walk-in business. The receiving dock was the staging area for the TV show and auction, a unique way to sell merchandise. Deal Time auctioned toys, furniture, appliances, clothes, and dry food.

The main thing was to have merchandise assembled and ready for the auction, which aired every night from 7 p.m. until midnight. They would auction ten items at a time. Phone operators would handle calls with bids. The show generated walk-in traffic, and customers would often recognize employees, which was fun.

Pallets of returned merchandise were sold by auction at wholesale warehouses, where Deal Time would bid on fully loaded pallets. It was amazing how many grass-filled, dirty lawnmowers that were used all summer had been returned to wherever it was purchased! I believe the customer-satisfaction mentality has helped develop spoiled American consumers who feel they are right under any circumstance. The corporate runaway goal to please puts customers in total control, to meet demands even if beyond reason. The motto "the customer is always right" is most commonly attributed to Harry Gordon Selfridge, the founder of the London department store Selfridges, around 1909. Did he really know what that meant?

Dirty lawnmowers were just part of the hodge podge those pallets brought in; most items were sellable. Space was often tough to find because most staff were unmanaged, so merchandise could get everywhere.

There was a lot of assembling of merchandise. I had carte blanche to manage myself and use the far corner of the facility to build up assembling and repair stations. This area was nicknamed "The Viper Lounge" because I was nicknamed Viper by the staff one night while we were out bowling. That night, they all used character names from Top Gun. Since I was the oldest, my bowling name was Viper.

All electronics had to be tested, a task in which I proved to be most diligent. My many carpet warehouse jobs operating a pole lift had trained me to pilot Deal Time's forklift truck.

Pleasing customers seemed to be low on the list of priorities. More than once, I heard the owners tell customers not to return. As they say, where the head points, the body will follow. When management treats people like that, employees often will too. Predictably, the customer service soon started taking a dive. Even though it was a tough place to work, I did the job the best I could, and the customers I served appreciated it.

I was the only one with weekends off. Everyone else had to work seven days a week. Things often didn't get done when I wasn't there, and items would sometimes not be prepared for the 7 p.m. auction. Owner/manager/bed-head tried to hold me accountable for this, but I replied, "You cannot blame me for lack of production on days I don't work." He said I'd need to start working weekends, reassuring me that I would still get my forty hours. I responded with a question: "So let me get this straight, you want me to work seven days instead of five for the same amount?" Deal Time refused to pay overtime. Once again, I could hear the unemployment clock ticking in my inner ear. For me, Deal Time morphed into Squeal Time.

Dumping trash was another issue. You can imagine how fast it would build up in a place like that. We had one trailer-sized dumpster that they would have to haul off and empty. I had a Nevada driver's license, so Squeal Time could avoid an out-of-town fee at the dump if I was driving the truck. Squeal Time never even offered a thank you when I took care of that.

It became evident that I was an odd one out. This did not bother me. I had money saved and could tell this business was pointing south. Behind the scenes, I saw how they behaved unethically. They treated their customers and employees poorly.

I knew time was ticking one night when I was on phones. It was simple: You answered the call and entered a bid under the caller's name. A Total Gym AbCrunch machine came up, and I'd been wanting one. Squeal Time never let staff purchase directly from the store. Rather, bed-head would say, "Just bid on it." I started bidding, but one person kept outbidding me. The bid got too high for me to want to continue. I told a coworker, "Man, some guy named Carson keeps outbidding me." She told me Carson was actually bed-head Squeal Time using a fake name to hike the bid price online from his laptop. Instead of just letting me buy this thing, he was inflating the bid to squeeze extra dimes. There was no way to catch on to this ploy if you were a bidder. I was working for a snake. It's funny how losing all respect makes your boss suddenly even easier to read. The ab-slider didn't sell, so what good did that do for them?

One day, owner/manager/bed-head informed the staff that a popular television network known for reality shows in the area was considering picking up Squeal Time. He told everyone that selling this auction to the network was a priority, so we were to feel free to be as entertaining as possible. I considered that a towering green light.

I was unpacking boxes when I came across two foam toy baseball bats. They were solid and light. In a rapid revelation, I rolled over two industrial-sized drum containers. I jumped up on the auction table and started banging beats on those large plastic drums—a joyful disruption of the entire place. When I was done, it went silent, marking a memorable moment in an otherwise crappy entry on the employment timeline. I figured, what the hell? They wanted more attention for the show so it could get picked up by a network. I made my contribution.

Pounding on those containers was my one-finger salute to Squeal Time Las Vegas. One day not long after, I was "given the night off." I knew what that meant, so I told a coworker I was going home early and probably getting fired. She doubted me. Sure enough, I got home and received a call that I wasn't needed anymore. I had my own choice words of farewell for them.

"What good could come of this?" One, including me at the time, might ask. Well, as I've been aiming to establish, few things in life are a total loss, even when they suck. At this job, I reinforced values I would not compromise. While I didn't plan to ever put this job on my professional résumé, I did get a few laughs when talking about it. For example, I found private Polaroids of owner/manager/bed-head's naked wife he'd left in a tool chest.

One night a few months later, I was feeling a bit bored, so I decided to check in on my pals at Squeal Time. By then, the auction was online only. I logged in as a bidder with the same fake name owner/manager/bed-head had used against me, Carson. I started making outrageous bids using the name Carson. It was a Triple 7 hoot watching him get excited about large bids and then lose his patience on camera when the new girls working there said, "Carson's on the phone!" He kept yelling, "No, it's not him!" I was able to enjoy at least twenty minutes of good old-fashioned prank calling the live auction online. It was no surprise they squealed away out of business not long after that.

Squeal Time was no doubt a job where you could wear blue jeans, as well as sport a bed-head. I was working on the shipping dock in the Nevada heat when I concluded, "I'm wearing shorts!"

Chapter 56

Halloween Mart

Las Vegas, Nevada, 2011–12
- Retail sales/expert on using useless knowledge
- Total income: $19,834.14

Craigslist advertised seasonal help at Halloween Mart in general labor. It was August, but Halloween Mart was ramping up to accommodate the coming weeks of masked madness. I cared for Trent still and could work part-time. I emailed a résumé and received a call to participate in their annual group hiring.

Halloween Mart was a year-round family business with a view of the entire Las Vegas strip from their receiving dock and parking lot. The showroom was small with lofty ceilings; they used every inch to display props, wigs, and both high-end and standard costumes. People will dress up for all occasions, and every holiday has its costume. Kids' costumes are sold all year. Halloween Mart generated a healthy amount of sales online as well.

The warehouse was connected to the sales floor in the corner, right past a makeup area where they held half of our run of the mill group interview. Arriving dressed to impress with two government-issued IDs was all it took to get hired. Not surprisingly, some did not pass the group interview.

With seasonal group hiring, the staff must be filtered out quickly. There aren't two weeks to train anyone; two weeks could be how long the job lasts. The real screw-ups won't make it past the initial screening. Sure enough, one woman kept asking questions and mentioning situations irrelevant to the group interview. She divulged personal information about herself to personalize the setting. The interviewer was visibly annoyed, so I spoke up. I raised my hand and asked the interviewer, "I'm sorry, could we continue the interview?" This was risky for me: blatantly changing the subject, suggesting time was being wasted. Trust me, I waited, but the sidetracking went too far, and if you deliver logic with a smile, it should be welcomed. In this case, the risk paid off, and we smoothly moved on. The idea for these interviews is to conduct them at a timed and focused clip. Do not prolong them or agitate others in the group by asking unnecessary questions! I could tell the woman who kept raising issues would not be brought on board.

The second part of the interview took us to the sales floor. The floor manager was a "white shirt," which I'll get to in a bit. She asked us basic questions. Her only pre-hiring task for us was to go around the shop and use three items to make a costume in ten minutes or less. It could not be an existing costume in a package. I put together something inspired by a customer's potential lack of time and money along with interest in mobility, which is how I presented it. Many guys don't have a costume until a few hours before a last-minute Halloween party. The floor manager understood my aim and was impressed by my Weird Al costume, which consisted of clear glasses, a curly wig, a red pleather sparkling jacket, and a rubber chicken. (If you aren't familiar with this ensemble, see "Weird Al" Yankovic's "Eat It" video.)

I was set to start the following weekend. When I arrived, many new hires were on duty. All wore bright orange shirts and the required black pants and black shoes. The managers wore white shirts, cashiers wore black, and the warehouse staff wore gray.

This was a delightful job! Many employees were young, single, and new in town. I made friends. The operation was hectic, and it required being reliable. We all wore an earpiece for communicating by a radio CB. Halloween Mart gave everyone laminated cards with squawk codes. The costumes were stored in the warehouse by letter and number sequences. For example, a sales-staff member would call an "attention runner," wait for a response, and then request an A3-H5 costume with "apple3-halloween5." I learned the code alphabet quickly by memorizing and repeating three letters a day until I got to Z.

All floor costumes were samples, which customers were encouraged to try on. Management felt sales would be better if people could fit the sample costumes first. It proved to be true. Each available costume and all of its sizes had to be on the floor as samples. You can imagine how messy and unorganized that could get. It was crucial to stay in your assigned aisle to help limit the chaos.

Halloween Mart wanted every sales staff member to upsell the costume's accessories. This came naturally to me. It required basic sales skills and listening to the customer. Plus, I still remembered the names and traits of many fictional characters from pop culture and Halloween lore; all of that trivial info floating in my head was now valuable. I worked an aisle for one day before being properly staged at the checkout counter. They had me working the wigs too. A wig and a wig cap facilitated instant upselling to costumes and original ways to talk to female customers.

Halloween Mart had printed cycle-count sheets that I familiarized myself with. They served to deepen my knowledge of the retail stock during slower periods by finding everything on those lists and confirming their identified quantities. This might include tracking down unaccounted-for quantities. Once I started to account for inventory, use the computer and accessorize the costumes, Halloween Mart had me, an orange shirt, working at the front counter permanently, which meant more hours.

At the same time, the white shirt owners brought in friends as "black shirt cashiers," some of whom seemed to view themselves as appointed favors to us for handling the Halloween craze. However, proper cashiering differs from being a clerk who just rings up whatever they're presented. It further entails being efficient with answers to questions; otherwise, the transaction can take twice as long.

I also proved to be useful with the graveyard props in the store's back corner. Expensive ones, too! Several were noise-activated with a clap. Working in the graveyard further let me float around and talk to customers, as well as help with the checkout line for samples. The line could often get lengthy, so I would explain to customers that others can't try on a sample costume being held in line. If a customer wasn't making a purchase, but still in line with a customer who was, I asked them to please step out. This could cut many lines in half, which mattered because customers who saw long lines might leave the store.

At first, I didn't always get the idea that the primary white shirt liked me that much. She'd often say, "You just think you are so funny!" I could tell she was thick-skinned, so I would reply, "Yeah."

When we finally closed on Halloween night, we had a meeting where the owners thanked everyone and handed bonuses to those who had stayed through Halloween night. They kept a handful of orange shirts for a couple weeks' worth of post-sale cleanup. On

November 1, "normal" life would resume until it was time to ramp up again the following summer. I was one of two Orange Shirts brought on permanently to work the off-season.

In assessing my own performance that first season, I felt that during the hectic times, I could shine through personal interaction with customers, but slower periods called for me to further refine and exhibit other skills. For instance, Halloween Mart was trying to build their customer database. I excelled at ensuring this because I could gather and enter names with organized precision. A customer using the same system ID for purchases made an enormous difference for efficiency. A store return with a recognized name was easier. Having contact info could allow me to locate a customer who might leave a bag behind. They may have even mentioned the hotel they were staying at, so having their name in the system could help us get their forgotten purchase to them.

During other stretches of downtime, Halloween Mart would ask me to write costume descriptions for their website. I was proficient at this, sitting at a computer composing hundreds of them over several weeks. Summertime was slow for Halloween Mart; however, I was just glad to have a job in air conditioning.

I had been getting night shifts with Las Vegas Parking. There were times when I worked at Halloween Mart from 1 p.m. to 8 p.m. and then valet parked from 11 p.m. to 7 a.m. Those were long days followed by sleepy Sundays.

When the end of the next August came into view, white shirt management instructed me to develop the graveyard. I really enjoyed it because the other sales staff let me do my thing and I was getting paid to decorate for Halloween! I determined which electronic props and devices still functioned. I arranged items so that all props could be turned on with a simple power-strip switch. I created Halloween themes with each grouping's items displaying SKU numbers and prices; retail merchandise can sell itself with properly tagged signage.

The graveyard was a dark corridor with the full display of props, black lights, and motion-activated Halloween gadgets. The graveyard's ceiling was low, and there was only a front and rear entrance. It was our own little haunted house. I had set up all the motion-triggered props to activate with one loud pop of a clipboard. I knew all the sweet spots for animating them and devised my own little joke. It would be quiet as customers cautiously walked through the graveyard. I would sneak to one of my sweet spots. The simultaneous pop of the clipboard and springing to life of the props made the customers freak out and then bolt. Shaking their heads and laughing, staff members would see me hiding by one of the sweet spots, and occasionally they would watch the scene unfold.

I was a Halloween retail rock star. I could run two registers at once: one on my left and one on my right. I knew the inventory back to front. I wore wigs, hats, light-up jewelry, and props, but not costumes. My favorite stunt was using latex makeup pieces to fake the appearance of wounds on my face or worms crawling out of my skin.

After I found a small karaoke machine in the warehouse, I used it to walk around the store and make announcements while wearing a Batman mask. In my best Batman voice, I'd say, "All costumes on the floor are samples; please keep them in their aisles." I would go outside to make announcements to people waiting in line as well. The karaoke machine gave me a great way to encourage customers to get the complimentary popcorn into their mouth instead of onto the floor!

That second season was just as busy as the first. Once, a customer who was a famous DJ wanted to get the best pirate costume. I got him into the most expensive costume and accessories. He said he would put me on a list for a big-time party where he'd be playing. I didn't make it to the party. He returned the next day and was like, "Dude, where were you?" I kicked myself for sure.

My rent was cheap, I lived close to work, and I was still playing music. I decided to take the general labor tour back to Phoenix, where my sisters Teresa and Janice were living.

Inventory management, register work, and customer service experience made more healthy additions to my résumé, accompanied by a reliable reference. Amped up for a final Halloween season, I was smooth sailing to my next port! Halloween day at the store, we set up an area with energy drinks and vodka in the warehouse for some fun after closing. It would be my last day there, and it was fantastic.

The required attire included sneakers if they were mostly black. I still had plenty of the necessary black pants from previous jobs. I didn't mind the dress requirement because wearing blue jeans in Nevada was too hot for me. Touring back to Phoenix, I knew the summers were slightly hotter than Nevada's. The idea of working in blue jeans was increasingly fading like an old pair of jeans.

Chapter 57

American Valet

Phoenix, Arizona, 2013–14

- Account manager/valet for the last damn time
- Total income: $36,332.50

I had money saved and a month to sell my stuff before touring on, which I did by having two garage sales.

Once again, Jen offered me room and board at her house. I always enjoyed staying with her and Trent. She was always accommodating, and it was never about money. I had time, but only a little; the job search was on. Eventually, I moved into a backyard casita as a live-in pet-sitter courtesy of Craigslist.

American Valet was advertising in the general labor section on craigslist.org. While in Nevada, I emailed my résumé and set up an interview for when I arrived in Arizona. American Valet managed parking throughout Arizona and branching to surrounding states.

The owner, Mike P., started the company in 1980 just like any other valet who said, "I can do this." American Valet was successful, employing many people. Mike was known in Phoenix and he had no problem telling people he was the owner and proud of it. American Valet had executive-level positions, insurance, and actual benefits. I would not have returned to valet parking if it didn't include advancement potential, and it was an easy job.

My interview was with a medical-accounts manager originally from Illinois. We went over the basics of valet service, and my experience was evident. Medical accounts are their own distinct parking category, and boosting tips is not necessarily the priority. Tips would be lower than those at bars and restaurants. The manager explained there were a couple of management positions, but they usually filled those from within. Still, he considered me for an assistant manager position at one of the hospital accounts because of my experience and interview. Working a medical facility would mean regular hours—even daytime ones! That would be great because valet parking often entailed nights and weekends.

I had to attend a new-hire orientation that was a true test of willpower! A three-hour orientation about valet parking. Man. Boring as hell was an understatement. I've concluded that these types of orientations must factor into the employer's screening process. I sat through it, answering a question here or there. The key was to do whatever I could to help keep it short.

Many new hires needed this orientation. People can assume that valet parking is simple. It can be—for those who practice common sense. This orientation was a policy reinforcement class, ensuring people understood why the most basic instructions were vital. Keys cannot get lost or locked in a car. Tickets must be used properly. How to inspect a vehicle before taking possession to park it was a critical step that had to be followed to a T. Almost every car out there is scratched up on all four corners, and allegations of damage by the valet are ready to be hurled. We were issued the required red American Valet embroidered polo shirts at this orientation. The company image was the polo shirt, navy blue pants or shorts with all black running shoes.

I next attended onsite training at the giant Banner Medical Facility. Hospital parking can be plentiful, but the front entrances usually benefited even further from having a valet service because we were often assisting the elderly, sick, and disabled. We did this to be helpful, not for tips. We understood why hospitals hired us.

The Banner account was busy enough for group training. I arrived early in uniform. Here I was again with a crew including numerous newbies. Now older, I realized that running Olympic routes and leaping park benches as I once had wouldn't be in this particular circuit. I did run though to and from each pickup and get all the doors for patients and visitors, even if it was for a car I hadn't pulled up.

The trainer at Banner was the account manager for St. Joseph's Hospital in central Phoenix, where I was being considered for an assistant manager position. Training with the account manager was my opportunity to sway the decision.

The trainer had to stay until the last trainee left. I offered to stay as well. There's no shortage of people wanting to cut out in such a scenario. He'd already been noting my work performance and ethic, and he knew I was ready for the job at St. Joe's. He said he would approve me. That's all it took.

I drove to the St. Joe's account Friday afternoon and observed the location from a distance to evaluate what to expect. St. Joe's was close enough for me to bike if necessary. Working there would be great for many reasons. One was that my sister Teresa was a surgery tech at St. Joe's. Of all the accounts I could get, I had a day shift at the same place! It was tough for us to coordinate regularly, but she and I managed to visit and even have lunch.

American Valet hired me to be one of two assistant managers. My shift was 5:30 a.m. to 1 p.m. The evening assistant manager worked from 1 p.m. to 8 p.m. The company reimbursed me for my phone usage. We pooled and divided tips based on an average hourly rate, which is the fairest approach.

I started the next Monday morning. It was December in Phoenix—chilly but not cold that day. Being a valet from the Midwest, I knew better than to stand outside in colder weather unprepared. I remember laughing because the other valets had to huddle around a propane outdoor heater. These are common in Arizona. I'd worked valet jobs with no heater in Chicago's dead of winter. I knew how to dress.

I was impressed by American Valet's custom valet stands, which housed a computer and secure key storage. The stands had to be reliable and able to withstand high winds and extreme heat.

We had a cashier and front-ticket guy who wasn't twenty-one yet, so he couldn't valet per the company's insurance policy. Cashiers collected the parking fee, were paid minimum wage and not eligible for tips. We still tipped, though, because the front-ticket person's demeanor can contribute to how much and how often valets get tipped.

American Valet had to hustle to keep the morning shift manned because of the early start. I had no problem with it once I got used to it. I began at 5:45 a.m., and the valet stand was to be open by 6 a.m. I was responsible for ensuring other entrances were up and running as well. If another stand didn't check in by a specific time, I had to open it until coverage was available.

Being done at 1 p.m. in the Phoenix summer is worth getting up at 4:30 a.m. I used to have a song: "In the Pool by 2, in the Pool by 2, the sun is out, the sky is blue, and I'm in the Pool by 2!"

I enjoyed Saturday and Sunday's peace of mind because the valet account did not operate on weekends.

One of the things I loved about valet parking was meeting so many different people. I remember a valet from Cuba raving about how working in America was a gift and telling how back home Cuban military jeeps had pulled into his neighborhood confiscating furniture from him and his neighbors. He felt Americans are so spoiled they don't even know it.

The busy St. Joe's account required good valets. Even though I hadn't valeted at a medical facility before, I understood what it was like be a patient. For example, no one had to tell me that people in wheelchairs or older people—especially those with walkers or canes—needed help opening doors. To employers of valets in such settings: If you must train prospective employees on this, you're wasting your time. I also knew not to get bent about not getting a tip because other patients and visitors frequently made up for it. We always wound up over minimum wage, and with day-shift valet parking, that was a win.

I had to manage the morning crew until the account manager arrived or when he was needed elsewhere. I could tell existing valets had a problem with me, which wasn't surprising. I tended to be a disrupter of ineffectual business practices. I didn't participate in pointless conversations at the valet stands, many of which were between guys trying to prove who knew more than the other. I quickly identified a few things that could be improved upon.

I needed help getting some valets on board with simple regulations. They walked for cars, a valet parking sin! They neglected opening and closing car doors and showed up late for shifts. This frustrated me. The basic-procedure slackers were younger guys who thought they knew the job better than me because they'd been working the account longer. Plus, the air was a bit bitter because my assistant manager position had been given to a new hire. I was confident it would all work out if I honored the company rules and stuck to my principles. I was in my thirties, and most of the valets working the different shifts were in their twenties. The few around my age had my back because they knew slacking cost us tips.

There was never a shortage of things to do, so I aimed to lead by example by walking the circle to collect any trash. I would even walk to the "other half of the circle" to assist with pick-ups and drop-offs that weren't in our valet domain. I saw great tip-worthy service opportunities being left on the table, and leading by example started showing this to the inexperienced employees. There were only a few but these choonts were costing me money by not doing the tip-growing basics. Money always wins, and I figured valets would comply if I sold the tipping factor. Other valets got the picture and started attending to car doors—and not just for females. When the account holder sees the valets performing this simple but meaningful gesture, it communicates unison, as if we're a platoon. It's like the 1950s gas station where a team came out and serviced one car. You can create that impression today simply by opening doors.

After about six months, American Valet offered me a Wednesday-night position as a new-hire orientation trainer that would not interfere with my assistant manager duties. They wanted someone to engage new hires for three hours, distribute uniforms, and collect new-hire paperwork. I would personalize the orientation by discussing previous valet experiences from Chicago, sharing pictures of my band, and highlighting all the things I was able to do while working with American Valet. In time, however, I realized they were enhancing the orientation position in a way I wasn't qualified for. I remember reading the ad for it recognizing that it just wasn't me. I was relieved when I had my Wednesday nights back.

I eventually learned how to use their valet stand computer software, so I could tell the cashier to clock out and go on break when he tried to eat his breakfast burrito at the valet stand ten minutes into his shift. Previous assistant managers had let this kind of stuff pass, not me. This cashier eventually gave notice.

I often reminded the valets that ours was not an entertainment account. For example, we had to be mindful of our conversations while people waited. We never greeted with, "How are you?" We worked at a hospital! The answer could be something the customer does not want to discuss. People could be going through a very difficult ordeal, so I trained valets to simply say "Hello."

Customers who refuse help are stubborn but could still use assistance. Hospital administrators were watching, so I told the guys to stand by the "I can do it" patient regardless. We often parked for people getting regular treatments, including chemotherapy. I tried my best to remember those people and retrieve their vehicles ahead of other customers, waiving any fee and never expect tips; they were usually generous.

The valets sometimes scoffed at me because I was active and earnest about the non-smoking policy on hospital grounds. Quite often, visiting choonts smoked on the hospital grounds. I couldn't believe smokers' rampant response to a non-smoking policy. Choonts would try to complain, but we were encouraged to inform violators of the policy. There was no way anyone under my management was breaking that policy or leaving the grounds to smoke. My stance on smoke breaks was "too bad."

Being an assistant manager had advantages, but it still required running as much as the other valets. By the weekend, I was usually beat. While still more accessible than the valet lots we had in Chicago, the lot at the hospital was far from the stand. I started wearing ankle wraps, but my ankles would eventually hurt like I'd never felt. I'd seen how managers spent scorching summer days doing paperwork sitting in air conditioning. There was no way I wanted to run around outside again the next summer. I wanted to get my own account. I had taken American Valet's manager training orientation before a position was open, so I was ready for when one was.

My opportunity arose during Mike P.'s personal baby, the Waste Management Open (also called The Phoenix Open) in Scottsdale. This world-famous golf tournament takes place every February. Upon hiring, every American Valet employee would agree to be available to work the Open, regardless of one's regular shift.

The Phoenix Open sparks a lot of new interactions among valets and managers. Through networking, many valets would work at other accounts with valets with whom they'd worked The Open. At the Phoenix Open that year, I met some of the company's higher-ups.

I had to pull a minimum of three separate shifts at the Open. They knew I had an account to open as well, so I was always dismissed early. Once again, I was ready with the proper attire. The Open is often sunny and warm at 3 p.m., but then the sun goes down. It may be Phoenix, but it's still February.

As a manager with American Valet, I was stationed at the entrance. It was a fun and easy stand to work because I encountered all the guests. Cars would arrive at sunset when the Open was over. At that time, many veteran managers then started turning away customers who didn't have parking passes but were willing to pay cash. We had plenty of parking spaces, so it struck me as an easy "yes sir!" Since tips were only for the runners, the higher-ups didn't care if service stopped. I did care, though, and I recognized the opportunity for further revenue while still accommodating customers who gladly handed over $20 bills that would increase the tip pool. I easily accepted twenty more cars. Once runners found out four hundred bucks had gone into the pool, parking vehicles without passes had way more support, including from regional managers who would make future decisions on who would get hired at their accounts. I couldn't help it: I wasn't going to turn money away. When Mike P. asked what was going on, I told him his right-hand guys had stopped taking cars. Mike P. knew increasing the tip pool made the runners happy. I made the impression I needed and eventually was offered an account to manage.

Around this time, I happened to pass by John C. Lincoln hospital in north Phoenix and thought it would be a fantastic location to valet. And go figure, days later a company-wide email went out seeking a manager for that account. I called the office right away and was immediately offered the new position.

The valet service at the new account was complimentary for hospital patients and visitors, meaning I wouldn't need to account for money. My responsibilities would include scheduling two other valets and keeping a daily record of ticket use on an Excel spreadsheet.

Operating hours were 8 a.m. to 5 p.m., Monday through Friday - in other words, perfect. At the same time, I'd never seen so many people parking in handicapped spots with blatant disregard, including plenty of choonts on their motorcycles. I would explain to a rider that he was blocking the painted section for wheelchair-accessible vans needing a side ramp. A part of me wished a van would pull up and extend the ramp right into the bike.

This Deer Valley location was the easiest managerial gig out there. The valet lot was visible from the stand and an obstacle-free cake-walk run. The John C. Lincoln medical account was as far north as it got for American Valet service within Phoenix limits. While managing it, I would joke that I was from the "north." No one bothered me "up north." It was such a quiet account that I managed for six months.

Another account-management opportunity arose at a major, busy medical facility. It was in Scottsdale = fancier cars and more money. A few managers were up for the job, which I had to interview for. I sometimes had to laugh at the faux decorum of such interviews. Why did I have to dress up and formally present myself at a company I already worked for—to boot, one that parked cars? I wanted to wear my valet uniform so bad.

The assistant regional manager for medical facilities had been training me to assume the Scottsdale Health Center account, but developing company cutbacks presented him with two choices: Be laid off or step into the Scottsdale position I had been offered. He busted his butt, so I thought it was lame they were considering giving him the axe. I couldn't blame or spite him for accepting the demotion from co-managing the medical division to running the single Scottsdale account. This is really where my perspective began to adjust. There was great potential they could eventually treat me the same way. Their cutbacks were the type of firings I'd grown to view as red flags.

I was pretty pissed but that soon morphed to indifference. I understood that for me to continue moving up in the business, I'd have to pucker my lips to kiss higher-up butt. Even though I'd held management positions, led orientations, and even launched out-of-town accounts, I wasn't impressing the right people. I realized that I wouldn't be one of their success stories.

On the upside, my résumé reflected two years of maintained management positions. I was becoming increasingly aware that running for cars was getting in the way of playing drums, which was a clear and present priority for me. I was faced with a decision. What could I do in the bigger picture on my terms?

I always browsed the general labor classifieds, even when employed. We significantly limit the odds of being hired if we wait until we're unemployed to search for a job. Oddly, grooming jobs advertised in the general labor section as well as the trades section.

Although I hadn't groomed pets in almost ten years, I still understood groomers made decent money and could quickly find work. The catch was you had to have your own tools.

If you have at least $1,000 in the bank, you're a thousandaire! It is a good mindset to be in when job searching. I was able to save the money to buy the right tools and the clipper-vacuum system I preferred, and practice grooming at a friend's boarding facility on Sundays. The key now was getting a full-time grooming job. Who would hire me? I wasn't even that good at it.

I was thirty-nine, and I aspired to live in California before turning forty. I contacted a Las Vegas landlord I rented from who had property in Alhambra, California, that I could possibly move into. I lined up a new grooming job and gave American Valet a two-week notice; two weeks is plenty to find a replacement for general labor jobs.

The Wednesday-night orientations I had going for a while had a casual vibe meant to be inviting to new hires. I was allowed to wear professional-quality blue jeans, accompanied by a collared shirt, and work in an air-conditioned office—always a cool perk in Phoenix.

My last day consisted of closing, leaving the podium keys locked inside itself, and exiting the parking lot. There was no goodbye, good luck, or thank you. I didn't expect much. And although it had been a respectable job, I would quit valet parking for good this time. My general labor tour would motor on to California.

Chapter 58

Fritzy's Pet Care Pros

Irvine, California, 2014
- Discontented mobile groomer/ignorer of red flags
- Total income: $7,239.57

My aim thus far has been to convey that most job experiences offer something to learn and take with us. Some jobs bedeck us with more positive traits than negative ones for carrying into our future. At Fritzy's Pet Care Pros, I picked up some of those positives, but the balancing scale we all want to work with was heavily tipped the other way.

Fritzy's operated within a vast radius of Southern California. They ran an ad in the general labor section of Craigslist and after submitting my résumé, I received a call from the owner. His name resembled Ned Flanders so closely that it was off by only one letter! This should have been my first detected red flag.

Flanders and I spoke for a long time, and I told him my plan to relocate from Arizona. The next step was a formal interview. I drove the five hours from Phoenix on a Friday after closing the valet stand.

The Saturday interview lasted over two hours. I detailed my mobile-grooming background, my time at Blum Animal Hospital, and the delivery jobs I'd worked. Going by Flanders' time spent with me; I thought my employment was certain. I was wrong.

Another red flag started rising with the ridiculous amount of necessary paperwork. Completing stacks about pay structure, regulations, procedures, and the grooming van required sweat and tears (no blood)—so much so that I decided to take them back to Phoenix before I proceeded. When I got home, I began my detailed review of the legal documents. Talk about asking for signatures! Enough to cramp even a drummer's hand. I told myself that some trouble with past hires must have prompted so many policies and release forms but I should have gone with my gut. The flags would only continue to form their long line in front of me.

After I completed the paperwork tower, we scheduled a ride-along with another groomer. I made a second trip to LA and met the groomer at his house, where his grooming van was parked on a public street. Flanders had given me the impression that I would be strictly observing. I later learned I was expected to perform tasks on the groomer's lengthy checklist. Trainees had to complete this company checklist to collect the commission-based salary. There was no way that all the tasks on the list could be done in a trainee's day.

After that ten-hour day, I had a long drive back to Phoenix. After a few days, I called Flanders to follow up. He said he couldn't hire me. This was confusing. I had given him pictures of grooms, and we had lengthy conversations in person and by phone. However, he claimed that I didn't perform the voluminous tasks on the checklist, nor did I have the approval of the ride-along groomer. I'd driven ten hours round-trip on two separate weekends for this. And yet I kept going.

We set up another ride-along with a different groomer. I drove to LA a third time and stayed in a hotel near her house. I was more hands-on the second time around, but I wasn't getting paid. I did the bath, nail trim, and blow-dry for all appointments—not easy. It was another long, eye-opening Saturday. The female groomer training me was pleasant but overworked. She had ten appointments that day. When you added that plus driving, you were looking at twelve hours if you were fast enough. She said that schedule was daily. Another red flag was waving.

I noticed that customers and my trainer had poor feedback about Fritzy's office staff. The most common was how frequently Fritzy's rearranged appointments that groomers had re-booked. Re-booking allowed groomers to make their own schedules and establish relationships with clients. Because of the variables, a re-booking schedule often took months to shape. Along the way, the office staff would reroute veteran groomers to new customers while sending new employees to serve regulars. This could be frustrating for both the customer and the groomer. It was another red flag flapping high in the wind, but I wanted to make the move to California, and if I had to job-search again, at least I'd be employed while I did it.

Flanders finally hired me. The company provided all the tools, as well as a phone. Oddly enough, even though they took their glacial time reviewing my paperwork and ride-along assessments, my van check-out felt rushed. This was a common vibe: It felt like Fritzy's was always operating with their hair on fire.

I initially worked fifty plus hours a week at minimum wage. I was playing in bands that paid here and there. I could pay my bills, but that was it. The van was easier to drive than a truck and trailer. Having office staff was helpful, but most of the time, it was disorganized with booking and routing.

The customers were friendly people. We had a lot of de-shed baths and simple grooms. All appointments were managed on a computer program that we, as groomers, could log into to see our appointments. This was convenient because I could check the schedule on my iPad throughout the day and before bed.

A considerable frustration in working with Fritzy's was going to bed at 10 p.m., knowing your next appointment was scheduled for 10 a.m., and waking up to find an 8 a.m. appointment that was a hike from your house had been added to your schedule!

Their scheduling was sporadic too. They'd book an appointment 40 miles away for 8 a.m. and then a second appointment not until 4 p.m. Two appointments! That left a lot of downtime in between, so I used it to learn music or call family. Usually, my day's last appointments were as far west as you could go before plunging into the Pacific. This required heading back east through LA between 5 p.m. and 7 p.m., a thirty-mile drive that took two hours. My employers didn't care that LA had brutal traffic and their ridiculous scheduling had me crawling and zigzagging through it. I spent three to five hours on the road each day.

I was sent to Compton several times. Yeah, that Compton. It was not a clever assignment by Fritzy's. I was a lone dude rolling through rough neighborhoods with a van full of equipment. It was unfortunate, too, because even though the area was disadvantaged, there were decent grooming clients who cared for their pets.

Another red flag had been rising up the pole too. I was only making minimum wage. Fritzy's paid 30% of the booking plus tips only after completing their lengthy certification checklist. Most mobile grooming companies paid 40% while stationary shop groomers got 50%. Understandably, providing the fully equipped mobile shop warranted less. I had to send pictures of my grooms to other Fritzy's groomers for approval. They rarely got back to me, and those who did were inconsistent as well as lukewarm or excessively critical. Some groomers tend to assess every cut as if it's for the Westminster Kennel Club Dog Show. Getting someone I never met to sign off on a picture I texted was not a productive system.

One example of the checklist items was a Schnauzer cut. Even though I completed the specific haircut for customer appointments, Fritzy's wouldn't credit my list because a senior groomer had yet to approve my photo of the cut. I repeatedly asked, "How can you send me to an appointment for a schnauzer cut when you haven't approved me for a schnauzer cut?" Flanders never had a sufficient explanation.

Another certification checklist item was a complete shave-down of a cat, including the head and paws, which is *never* done. Beyond being risky for the groomer, it can injure the cat. Shave-downs are 99% lion cuts, leaving the face, head, paws, and mane unshaven. No reputable groomer performs a complete shave-down on a cat and having it as separate from lion cuts was just stupid. When I raised this issue with Flanders, he responded, "Can't you have a friend let you do it?" I explained the potential for injury and that it was *not* a standard practice. It's irresponsible to shave someone's cat in that way! At this point, at least in my mind, Fritzy's became Shitzy's.

Creeping through ninety-minute rush hour traffic to our mandatory 7 a.m. Wednesday meeting was a colossal wrench in the machine. Rife with irrelevance, the meetings unnecessarily cost Shitzy's expensed employee gas and mileage. I recall only one Wednesday meeting of worth. We were reviewing clipper maintenance, and I picked up a few useful tips on clipper repair.

Shitzy's was running so poorly that the entire staff became disgruntled. During one of the many pointless other meetings, I pointed out that no one in the room was making more than minimum wage. As usual, a question of substance seeking an accountable answer was addressed with "let's have a private meeting after this, and we can talk about it one-on-one." The old deflection was a trademark Flanders move. Red flag.

They performed drawn out van inspections at these meetings. Shitzy's would penalize groomers by taking money from their check according to an arbitrary review of van inventory and cleanliness. I can't overstate how low this is. If the supplies were off by even one item, such as a toothbrush, or noted something such as loose hair in the van, you paid a $5 fine for each infraction! In some cases, the source of the different count could have been their own often unreliable accounting system—you just couldn't know. Accountability matters at any business, but if an employer dings employees for clerical mistakes or occasional oversights by automatically deducting from their paychecks, the employees will quit. Man, the red-flag brigade was just signaling. EMPLOYERS: DON'T MESS WITH THE MONEY!

My van often wasn't inspected in time before the meeting concluded, so I was usually late to the first appointment. I knew I would not keep this job and started searching anew after a month and a half.

Employees had to work their regular day off during the week of a major holiday. Grooming is a physically demanding job, and an occasional extra day off is justifiable for rest. Christmas red flags were wildly whipping and snapping.

Christmas Eve that year was on a Wednesday. Flanders decided our Christmas Party would be held at the Wednesday 7 a.m. meeting. Yes, a Christmas party at 7 a.m. on Hump Day. What a joke. On top of that, instead of bonuses, Flanders gave us candy made by his family with a grab bag full of cheap items such as a note pad with a golf-club pen, probably from somebody's junk drawer.

On that Christmas Eve, they would book appointments up until 4 p.m. instead of 5 p.m. Woopty-doo! Sure enough by the time

I left the lame Christmas party, I was late for my first appointment, which would then mess up the rest of my day.

Before heading to my last appointment, I phoned the office to report the newly inspected van had been making a loud, grinding clank. The brakes appeared to be the problem, I told them I didn't think continuing the 100 plus–mile trip would represent a decent IQ. They asked me to pull over so they could hear the sound over the phone while the van was rolling! I lowered my eyebrows, pursed my lips, and considered how I might stand outside the van with the phone while driving the van. Their next Mensa-worthy suggestion was to have me wave down a passing motorist on the Christmas Eve LA highway. Then, I should ask that motorist to stand on the shoulder and hold my phone on speaker while I drove the van by. This, the office put forth, would help to verify the sound.

But wait—there's more. They further insisted that we did not want to lose the appointment to which I'd been driving. Having me break down far from home on Christmas Eve was the lesser possible pain point. As it turned out, the customer, a retiree, didn't even care if her appointment was that day. Getting her in before Christmas wasn't necessary. I called the office one last time to swap out a van, but Flanders wanted me to drive the current one home. I turned the stereo all the way up to drown the grinding clank.

So that, my friends, was Christmas Eve 2014 for me. I worked twelve hours for minimum wage, a note pad, a schlocky pen, some kids' Happy Meal junk, and homemade candy I tossed.

I had appointments booked for the day after Christmas, and the van still had to be fixed. Flanders demanded that the Shitzy's in-house mechanic drive to my house and fix it on Christmas Day. I told him that mechanics couldn't be out on our street doing a brake job on Christmas; they needed a proper garage. Flanders insisted they could be out there.

So, I waited for the mechanic on Christmas who never showed up until the next morning claiming ignorance on my phone number—after waking me up for the van key, of course. I was more pissed than a corkboard dancing with a cactus.

The mechanic soon realized that the entire brake drum had melted; the van would have to be towed. We swapped the van he'd driven to my house. In the short time I worked for Shitzy's, I switched vans five times, so I couldn't buy a city vehicle sticker, which was required to park on the street where I lived. I hated changing vans. They all had different little quirks with things that did and did not function. I would figure out how to get something operating to my liking and then lose it because the van was down for repair again. In three days, I had seen enough lack of logic and respect to replace the Christmas red flags with a white one. I had to find another job.

I got to where I didn't even care if I was fired or if any motorists were to call the office and complain about my driving. I ditched appointments I didn't like. When I was done with my last appointment, I headed straight home regardless of the time of day.

Mobile grooming in LA sucked and was going to continue to suck. I decided my next job search would be limited only to positions at groom shops. I even investigated a valet company despite having told myself I'd retired from the trade.

Craigslist advertised a bather position at a grooming shop just east of Alhambra in West Covina. I called the number while in the middle of an appointment for Shitzy's and was asked to interview the next day. I called in sick to Shitzy's and the shop hired me.

Getting hired halfway through the day was thrilling! My roommates were happy for me. I called Shitzy's, but Flanders was unavailable. I told the office to cancel any appointments they had booked for me and to have Flanders call me when it suited him.

When he called six hours later, he knew what was up; the conversation was quick. Flanders said he would deduct a $200 pick-up fee from my last check if I didn't deliver the van back to Irvine for inspection within a few days. When I got to Shitzy's shop, the office staff gave me the cold shoulder from hell. They kept me waiting while they leisurely inspected the van. They even wanted me to return the hat I was issued. Kind of gross when you think about it.

One of the mechanics finally said, "So you're outta here too, huh?" I sneered, "I can't deal with Stupid Flanders anymore." He got the reference, wondered why he hadn't thought to call him "Stupid Flanders." They understood. The turnover rate was a peak that'd sailed off the chart, and these mechanics seemed tired of watching the main source of income go out the door.

Although it'd been a lousy job, I learned and explored Southern California's major roadways and towns. It got me back into the flow of grooming and gave me a catalyst to move to LA with a dash of health insurance.

I was excited to be done with Shitzy's and start my next chapter at a single location. I celebrated that weekend with a new job starting on Monday.

Stupid Flanders didn't reflect his blue jean attire. He may have worn them but he was not cool. Given the weather was always warm in California, I most often wore black shorts with a standard black short-sleeve grooming smock: perfect.

Chapter 59

West Covina Grooming/ Glendora Pet Spaw

Glendora, California, 2015
- Amateur groomer/low man on the totem pole
- Total income: $960.00

When I arrived for my interview the shop owner went back to her husband for a moment and said, "This is Charlie, our new groomer." That was reassuring considering I was willing to be a bather for minimum wage in order to get away from Shitzy's. From then on, the interview was more like brief training. She asked if I would start the following Monday. I replied promptly "yes," and neither of us was concerned about whether I'd give Shitzy's a two-week notice.

It was such a relief starting a new job in the opposite direction of LA's morning traffic. I cruised at 65 mph while the other side inched in gridlock. The sailing was the same on the way home.

When I arrived at West Covina Grooming for what I thought would be a simple bathing position, I realized what a small operation it was. The groomers all shared clients and split all tips through a tip pool. All dogs or cats were dropped off in the morning and picked up between 3 p.m. and 5 p.m. Not my preference, but it's the only way to groom twenty to thirty dogs daily. Many pet owners don't want to leave their pets all day. Others didn't like their pets being around that many animals. Staying at the shop for that many hours put some pets under extra stress. I worked half a day and wondered whether I'd made a mistake. The working conditions were tight, and the hours were just pull-time.

They operated a second, larger facility twelve miles north called Glendora Pet Spaw. They asked me to head up there and help out. Although slower, the Glendora shop was much nicer with less competition for grooms.

Glendora Pet Spaw had excellent equipment and supplied all the grooming tools, which was rare. I was glad to not have to bring my tools in. They wouldn't have wanted me using my separate vacuum system.

Their main groomer at Glendora Pet Spaw was good, as well as tolerant of my ways. She taught me basic scissor finishes and proper blade-size use. I would have to re-learn how to clip hair using forward motion without the vacuum attachment.

In the first few weeks, my skills improved. The main groomer seemed happy with my work, which I completed almost fully, save for some final additions. She knew she could finish in a few minutes whatever was left. Because so much was done by the time she was needed, we could still take in a lot of grooms. She preferred that efficiency over drama any day.

Typically, a bather will clean and dry a pet for the groomer before it gets a haircut. I preferred bathing dogs whose hair I cut and never minded doing that part of the appointment. One problem was the shop paid hourly. Under their scenario, the pay was the same whether you groomed five dogs or two. They would have me come in between 9 a.m. and 10 a.m. and then send me home randomly, sometimes right after I got there.

Saturdays were always busy, but even then, I made only a day's pay at minimum wage. Despite having earlier said that tips were split through a pool, they refused to distribute them at this shop, now claiming instead tips were for refrigerated beverages. At first, I didn't mind because I was glad to be done with Shitzy's. After a while, however, having tips withheld became an unhealable sore.

One day the co-owner wife claimed the other new groomer and I were amateurs and not on par with their professional grooming standards. She held her hand at her shoulder's height and said they were "up here." Then she lowered her hand to her waist level and said the two of us were "down there." She repeated, over and over, that everything they did was "professional" and "industry standard." I responded by asking, "Isn't paying groomers a commission and letting them keep their tips industry standard?" Naturally, this elicited silence, but I couldn't help it. It's tough to listen to someone quoting from one book while acting out another.

When I got home later that day, I looked up their Yelp reviews. I typically don't base my assessments on one bad review by an unsatisfiable customer. However, if I had read this operation's reviews earlier, I would have gained greater insight. Multiple customers seemed to take issue with the business's "professional" qualities.

The organ music of my employment carousel turned back on and the pole of the horse I was riding started to move. I checked-in on good old Captain Craigslist and its partner General Labor and Trades, finding an ad for a Pasadena grooming shop seeking full-time help. All applicants had to know how to use clipper-vac systems or be willing to learn!

After being hired I called Glendora Pet Spaw. With giving notice in mind, I explained they didn't have two weeks' worth of work for me. A "maybe I'll work today, maybe I won't" scenario with them would cost me money. With my new job, I could start the next day. The co-owner husband understood.

Later that day, I called Glendora Pet Spaw's main groomer to thank her for teaching me the finishing touches for shop-based grooming. Those enhanced scissor skills would follow me to my next groom-shop position and would help me provide professional quality grooms. She wished me luck. The withholding of tips alone would have been enough for most groomers to leave that job feeling bitter.

Because they had a bather at times, and a low flow of business, I could see how some people might wear blue jeans—until the hair got all over them. I don't recommend working at a groom shop in blue jeans!

Chapter 60

My Pet Garden

Pasadena, California, 2015

- Groomer
- Total income: $17,687.60

The shop was called My Pet Garden, and they offered pet daycare as well as boarding. When I arrived, customers were being served so patience was protocol, as it always should be.

The manager did the interview outside. I had brought good before-and-after pictures, which are essential to applying for grooming jobs. After interviewing me, the manager introduced me to the owner, who mostly screened me for reliability and likelihood of being a meth addict.

They wanted to get someone for the evening appointments ASAP, so having me in the following day for a test groom was next. For a small operation, they handled their workload well. Their clipper vacuum system was to order the attachments and retrofit your clippers to a standard shop vac. That was a little concerning to me because the beauty of my personal clipper vacuum was its speed-control dial that allowed low, quiet settings. A lot of pets are scared by vacuums, especially cats. To me it seemed that two or three groomers operating shop vacs at once could get loud.

The test grooms were simple, small dogs. They paid 50% commission plus tips for my test grooms. That is what's supposed to happen! They wanted me to start right away.

Their full-time evening groomer was vacationing for two weeks, so after 5 p.m. I had the groom shop to myself. Things changed slightly when the other evening groomer returned from Thailand. Her thick accent was hard for me to understand. One time when trying to get a dog under control, she was calling out, "No, Rucky, no, Rucky!" The dog's name was Lucky. I don't think he was being difficult; he was having trouble deciphering too. I still LIQ (laugh inside quietly) about that whenever I meet a pet named Lucky. *No, Rucky!*

I worked full-time, including Sundays but not Saturdays, which are usually status quo in the grooming profession. That was for the best, because they had a very busy Saturday system I couldn't keep up with. Another thing was that if I played on a Saturday night I didn't have to stress getting off work on time. Fortunately, Sunday was a short, usually quiet, low-key day with a later 10 a.m. start.

We offered cat grooming too. Groom shops take these appointments because they can charge $80. Mobile grooming appealed to many cat owners, so it was no surprise when the other cat groomer and I discovered we both had horror stories to share from working for Shitzy's. She got a kick out of the nicknames Shitzy's and Stupid Flanders.

Groomers were more responsible for cleaning duties than I was used to. We divided those, making it easier. On a rare slow day, we were expected to stay busy with cleaning. I usually wound up with six to eight pets to groom, making the day productive.

We seldom had downtime. Finding time for lunch was a necessary challenge. Grooming while hungry made me impatient. Patience is necessary when grooming pets.

The shop emphasized that we follow the appointment notes. I didn't like secondhand information because the front staff would take in grooms we couldn't do. For example, one owner might bring in a matted-down pet thinking it didn't need shaving. The front staff would say OK to the impossible haircut. We'd then have to call the customer and inform them it's shave-down time. We wound up doing the shave-down, and the owner complained at pick-up that they were told differently at drop-off.

For new client appointments, I insisted on delivering my finished groomed pet to the owner upon pickup to ensure satisfaction. Doing this prompted a tip. All tips were split up in an hourly cash pool. Many people were working there, and the customers were tipping everyone.

Even though I was enjoying this job, one reason I knew it wouldn't last was because of the facility, which was tight and loud. They gave naughty daycare dogs their timeouts in the groom area, which equated to "here you go, groomers—add a barking dog to the mix."

Their pet boarding meant pet feeding, and that took place in cages located in the grooming area. Imagine trying to groom a cat with several hungry dogs barking within feet. Quite often, I started my day cleaning the overnight boarders' now-unoccupied cages: not a groomer's job, but the choice was clear it or smell it.

I wouldn't do monkey work. I had to draw the line. They tried skywriting the old business adage "if you got time to lean, you got time to clean" on me, but that's a no-fly zone for commissioned workers.

If there was a rare slow day, I chilled. Don't get me wrong—I did the basic cleaning expected of us, but I wasn't going to deep-clean. That belongs in the domain of hourly pay. That's why I learned an independent trade and bought the tools to ply it.

I was amazed at how many dogs in California had fleas. This was my third grooming job in the state, and each one included many matted dogs with fleas. The pet owners typically didn't tell us. How does a person not know their dog has fleas? On a personal level, those grooms are always the most satisfying. Yes, they are lengthy, gross, and difficult, and they require tedious hair removal. Still, it's a joy to see the dogs emerging cleaned up, feeling 100% better, and wagging their tail. These are grooming's real rewards.

My Pet Garden held twice-monthly dental clinics, which impressed me. A vet tech would come into the shop and perform an anesthetic-free dental on any pet. She could simply lay it in her lap on the floor and scale its teeth. It was pretty amazing to see.

The shop's regular foot traffic could sometimes make grooming difficult. A pet being groomed will look for anyone to take it off the table. Staff members would walk by and meddle with a groom in progress by petting and kissing the pet. Trust me, it's not *you* they want—it's freedom!

I worked at this job for the rest of my stay in California and learned a lot about breed cuts. My Pet Garden helped me improve my skills further. At this point, I stonewashed the idea of wearing blue jeans to work. My dry-fit shirt under a standard short-sleeve grooming smock accompanied by light-fabric hospital scrub pants perfectly serves while maintaining basic work attire's casual vibe. Shorts are not considered safe shop wear.

LA is huge and spread out. It had taken me fifteen years of living in Chicago before the city's neighborhoods and inner workings became more intrinsic to me. I wasn't planning to stop the tour for the same duration sowing a life to be reaped in LA. By this point, half of my immediate family were living in Phoenix. I wanted to be closer to my nephew Trent as well. I had decided to take the general labor tour back to Phoenix.

Before my California move, my sister Teresa had referred me to a doggie daycare and boarding center called Scottsdale Doggie Suites. It helped me get back into grooming, and I worked there on Sundays before moving to California while managing the valet stand at John C. Lincoln in Phoenix. While I was in California, Scottsdale Doggie Suites announced they were moving into a larger facility. I contacted them and lined up a job for my return to Arizona; that is why I am including their chapter next instead of earlier.

I gave My Pet Garden my two-week notice at the start of November. I simply explained family was most important and I was moving back to Phoenix. They understood, and I agreed to finish out November. I was nearing my last day when Tuesday, November 24, 2015, hit me like a ton of bricks.

A self-rule of mine when I was working had typically been to not check my phone until lunch. I was particularly strict about this when valet parking. On November 24, I checked my phone at lunch and saw missing calls, texts, and voicemails. I went outside and called my brother Greg, who told me that my other brother Fred had suffered a cardiac arrest and was on life support. One can never be prepared for this. Fred had been down without a pulse for almost twenty minutes before paramedics arrived. I was stunned. I returned to the shop pale as a ghost and had to leave. Everyone there immediately offered help. Packing up to go was a seemingly impossible challenge that day. It felt like I'd never done it before.

I remember wondering what the hell I'd been doing that morning while my brother lay on the floor with no pulse. The relevance of grooming a dog rapidly shrank to the size of a sand grain. Halfway across the country, my brother had been struggling for life. I felt sick.

I flew from LAX to Chicago two days later on Thanksgiving Day and spent a week in a hospital waiting room. After nine days with Fred still on life support, I flew back to California on a Monday night and picked up my belongings at home and my tools at My Pet Garden, where I had a chance to say goodbye and thanks. I then drove from LA to Phoenix on Tuesday night, and LA receded behind me. I took my time. I had to. I needed a long drive to ease my mind.

I arrived in Phoenix the following Wednesday morning and immediately booked a flight back to Chicago for the next day. I would keep my belongings at my dad's in Surprise, Arizona, until I figured out my next move. I was alone in the house. That Wednesday night included my first real sleep in over a week.

Early on Thursday morning, I awoke to my sister Teresa's call: My brother Fred was gone.

Chapter 61

Scottsdale Doggie Suites

Scottsdale, Arizona, 2016–17

- Groomer/seeker of logic in an illogical place
- Total income: $33,987.64

After my brother was buried, I stayed with his family for all of December 2015. I returned to Phoenix and once again, Jen offered me rent-free living. She had gotten Trent a puppy, Trek, who was sixteen weeks old and now she had a dilemma. Who would care for this puppy? She worked, and Trek couldn't be left alone. I had saved money and was in no hurry to return to work. Scottsdale Doggie Suites (SDS) was still under construction. I stayed with Trek during the day for about a month. A puppy is the best remedy for grief. When someone dies, there's joy in new life. I loved that dog.

For the first time since turning fourteen, I had no interest working. For some people, work can get them through a tragedy. I didn't want to go back to normal: That felt as if it would have been a disservice to my brother. At the same time, the thought of telling people my story and explaining the gap in work history gave me unease.

When I was ready, a simple phone call was all it took to return to SDS, who was coincidentally finishing up construction for the new location. I found a residence in Scottsdale close enough to take a bike path to work.

The new facility was 8,000-square-feet with plenty of suites for dogs. Each spacious suite had thick glass doors as well as drywall. I liked that dogs wouldn't be in cages. I did have concerns with the location. For starters, the first thing I noticed was there was nowhere to walk the dogs. I didn't inquire about it; I thought they would ensure that dog-walking was possible. They sold the main play area as where the dogs "relieved" themselves.

The huge groom shop was in the back. I especially liked the pens where I kept the dogs for grooming. They were open on the top, with three secure sides and a front gate. The dogs weren't enclosed in cages and bonding with the pet was much easier. I could get in there and let them get familiar with my scent. I welcomed customers into the grooming area because the most common feedback was that people needed to learn what was happening in the mysterious back room.

I set the grooming area up how I wanted, including a drying room with a table and the ability to secure pets. The fire exit was in the far corner. Management often said they would build an outdoor play area with a splash pad as well. Although it sounded encouraging, I dreaded it because I knew once they did that, there would be a lot of foot and paw traffic, and when you're grooming, the opening and closing of doors can distract. Building out a splash pad, however, would take money and time.

Scottsdale Doggie Suites had trouble getting current groomers to take additional appointments once the day started. I never understood this, as most add-on appointments were simple go-home baths. That's easy money. After a few days at a boarding facility, a dog needed a bath—not a full-service bath, but a freshen-up. Management preferred having me on Sundays to ensure pet owners that paid for a go-home bath were ready to be picked up first thing Monday. No Saturdays dude!

After a month, I initiated a meeting with the other groomers at a centrally located bar. It was good because we all clarified several things. This simple meeting allowed us all to speak to one another freely at a strictly staff level. Pricing was the most confusing part of the grooming service. It had too much nickel and diming, so I put together a basic three-tier menu of services with easy-to-understand, competitive pricing. I saw no reason to charge extra for standard grooming practices.

The only extra charges I kept were for de-matting and for large dogs that get a shave-down only twice a year. If the customer thinks the price is too high, let them go. It's only two days' worth of earnings and a lengthy appointment.

I would need to acclimate to the new computer system: a bit of a task. It included grooming-history notes I could look up for each pet, which was helpful. I had to enter the charges and update notes for each appointment. The computers were in the front lobby. To use them, I had to wait until there weren't any customer transactions taking place.

Those first few months had a lot of downtime. I could have a long lunch and go shopping. If anything came up, I'd get a text. I would give customers a tour of the facility. I tried to answer phones when I could as well.

I had a key for staying late. I would often come in after closing to touch up the groom area. Grooming was its own separate operation. I was able to listen to my choice of music all day and wasn't bothered by anything else. Occasionally, I'd have to move a dog that was barking from a suite behind the groom shop to one farther from my work area.

A common problem could be having appointments several hours apart. That was frustrating, especially when the customer had no preference and was flexible about the time. I often had to double-check whether I was waiting for a dog already onsite because grooming appointments weren't always marked as boarder or daycare pets. There was no reason to put off grooming a boarded pet that was leaving that day. Management wanted the pet to get playtime, but owners often called to pick their pets up earlier than scheduled, so in my view, it was best to groom an outbound dog ASAP.

I really didn't like that the dogs didn't get walked. Allowing them to relieve themselves in the play area went against their proper housebreaking. Dog walks could be done in the front, and that was ultimately where they wound up, but property owners prohibited dogs from walking on that grass. It had to be done though. When a dog is trained to go outside, it will hold it until it no longer can. Not walking them was a poor way to care for boarders. Plus, it was just plain gross. Scottsdale Doggie Suites didn't have overnight personnel, and when they closed early on Saturday, no one was back until 9 a.m. Sunday. You might imagine what awaited the Sunday-opening staff.

Even with some of my concerns, I was thinking long-term about this job. There was a lot of potential for grooming. I liked the clients and built a good rapport with many grooming customers. Loveable dogs came in and out daily, which was always a reward. I started keeping an online album called "Groomed Pets."

I noticed a high staff-turnover rate. The complaints were the same for past and present employees alike. Eventually, I was the only groomer left. When I realized this was how it was, I avoided any situation or conversation concerning employees, pets, or customers that did not involve grooming. It was the smarter, safer way of working among drama. I was proficient at grooming, and it was providing me income.

When they finally completed the outdoor play area they'd been telling people about, as much as I wanted to be positive, I wasn't. I've already mentioned the potential new distractions to grooming. The door to the groom shop was big and metal and it slammed when it opened and closed. The dogs flinched every time.

With the play area open and active, dogs often stood outside the back door and barked all day long. The grooming space went from uninterrupted and quiet to the opposite. The outdoor area was good for the dogs, but it too was not well-maintained. Poop wasn't picked up. Fly swarms developed. It got gross.

I often arrived at the groom shop with neglected excrement on the shop floor. I later discovered the main culprit was the facility manager. I can tell you this: Beginning the day cleaning poop is the dictionary definition for a crappy start.

Another brewing problem involved available terminals. I had to use the computers up front to close out grooming sales. When it was my time for that, I ran into much resistance, contradiction, and conflict, including drama not worth writing about. I just knew I had to find another job.

Scottsdale Doggie Suites did have a genuine love for pets, but after a year, I realized the problems would always continue. It was time to get back on the carousel. At some point it had to let me step off in the right place, right? I will never regret interacting with the dogs: the best part of the job. I invested in the multiple pairs of scrub pants and lightweight workout shirts that I would continue to groom in. Thank goodness Arizona has many thrift stores!

One morning, the facility manager called me crying and packed my ear with her life problems blaming her work-related stress on me. I lay there speechless, half awake, listening to this jargon. After she finally got it all out, I hung up, now wide awake, I went right to Captain Craigslist.

The next time I saw the facility manager at SDS; I gave her my delayed reply to her rant: "May 5th." She asked what that meant. I said, "May fifth is two weeks from today. That'll be my last day." I don't know if that's the response she was looking for, but it was the response I gave. She looked down and walked away, and we never spoke again.

After completing my last day, I packed up and departed without any words; a rarity for me. I met up with my dad for Cinco de Mayo to celebrate yet another chapter destined to appear right here—and of course to celebrate with margaritas and tacos the Mexican army's victory over French forces at the Battle of Puebla on May 5, 1862 (for the history buffs out there). I didn't care that I didn't have a job lined up and that I was still riding the horsey on the fun-park carousel.

Chapter 62

Man's Best Friend

Scottsdale, Arizona, 2017–18, 2019–22

- Groomer
- Total income: $28,728.00

While dissatisfied working at SDS, I did a test groom at Man's Best Friend on my day off. The hiring decision came down to me and one other. They hired the other groomer. It was a professional decision, and I respected it.

I kept an eye on Man's Best Friend even though I noticed a high turnover (cue whipping red flag). After I quit SDS, I texted Man's Best Friend to see if they were hiring. They responded, "Can you start this Saturday?" I said, "Yes!" I came in that Saturday to a full day. I was willing to work Saturdays, which was all they could offer then. Working four fully booked Saturdays each month would cover my rent! Eventually I'd get days during the week.

They were closed on Sunday and Monday, so I knew I would always have those days off. The shop was spacious. Tubs and drying equipment stayed in the back area. Eye hooks were drilled into the floor to attach leashes for cageless grooming. Customers liked to walk in and see their freshly groomed pet relaxing on a towel, while still secure.

The shop's size was just right and easy to keep clean, and music was always playing. There was no boarding or daycare, nor were there cats. I could groom my sister Teresa's dogs there after closing as well. It hadn't been an option when I'd worked for SDS, and I'd felt terrible that she'd had to bring her dogs to another groomer when it's what I could have done for her under different circumstances.

I knew my grooming skills weren't as good as other groomers. I was slow, and most of my cuts were regular utility cuts based on the pet owners' preferences.

I preferred to do my own baths for dogs, but the shop manager, who wasn't a groomer, insisted on bathing dogs. This only helped if the bathing was correct, which it was not, and didn't interfere with customer service, which it did. At first, I was a little put off, but I decided to work with him on it. He paid us a commission on the appointments he did baths for, which was generous. I even told him I didn't expect to get paid for bath-only appointments that he did, but he persisted. He figured that he wouldn't have booked the bath without having the groomer available to do the finished or clinical work.

Man's Best Friend diligently confirmed the next day's appointments. A necessary practice for any appointment-based service. We groomers divvied up the checkout process. I have often found that people will do for you what you do for them. Lunch was provided on busy days, and my flexibility was appreciated. I was willing to work on days with just one booking and accept same-day or last-minute bookings. In turn, I could leave early to play music, and they even gave me a nice Christmas bonus.

I continued loading pics from the shop into my online "Groomed Pets" album. It remained an excellent format for presenting before-and-after pictures of my work. I could direct anyone to photos. Online albums are valuable for anyone with a skill-based trade. Tools to promote them are right there waiting for us!

I wanted the manager to be present at check-in for all clients who had matted dogs. People could get upset and offended if you informed them their matted dog had to be shaved. Some dogs can become matted by going into a pool or shower and not getting brushed after. That's neglect.

Many customers insisted that I "brush the dog out," even after I explained their pet's dreadlocks can't be brushed out! Most people who bring in matted dogs usually understand what the pet needs. The ones who don't, typically need a manager to tell them what they don't want to hear. I sent these folks straight out the front door. Some people who were turned away threw a fit, gave poor online reviews, called back to speak to the owner, and claimed the groomer was rude. Come on! You neglected the dog's coat, not me. You can't wash and wax a rusty car and expect the rust to be gone. It has to be removed.

If smelly dreadlocks in your dog's coat don't displease you, let me share from my experience that most matted dogs have blinding clumps of crust on their eyes and fecal chunks stuck to their back end. I guarantee that if you see what I remove from ears, you'll further understand what can propagate on a pet. Unfortunately, unless a customer personally witnesses the pet's entire gunk-removal process, they just won't believe you. When a dog has these conditions, I can't take the pet owner's concerns for appearance seriously. They should rather accept a shave-down that frees the dog's dirty, itchy skin that hasn't been exposed to air in months. These owners groom their pets infrequently, so if they resist or dislike such suggestions, losing them as customers is not a major loss.

There are exceptions. I've groomed matted dogs belonging to elderly people who struggled to keep up with grooming. In other cases, the dogs have been either rescues or super difficult pets that got highly stressed being groomed, leading the owner to neglect the procedure.

With this shop, we had a lot of no-shows without notice or explanation. These are challenging problems because you want to criticize the customers who do that, but you can't. If the pet owners reschedule, it's workable. I started tracking no-show appointments and charging for the missed dates the next time the customers came in. Being a key holder, I could have had those who missed appointments come in later in the day or after-hours when the manager had left. That was too much effort for the shop manager, who would rather let it go.

Things started getting bad when the manager spent more time doing other groomers' baths than being a manager who could lead and delegate. Potential new customers would enter and want to discuss bringing in their pet. The shop manager was busy washing and drying dogs in the back area behind a closed door. It started becoming untenable when he continued paying the other groomer for the bath-only appointments he completed himself while telling me he had no dogs for me on slower days.

I would come in after a day off to find there had been missed calls for changes or bookings that impacted my schedule. On other occasions, he lost his cool over minor setbacks. I began to doubt his troubleshooting skills and to question my long-term commitment.

The manager often commented that he "doesn't get a paycheck." I'm not sure what kind of salary he negotiated! He apparently was overlooking that he was paying the other groomer for work he performed. He picked up and dropped off pets for customers without fees or an organized system. His temper could flare at busy times as well, which is detrimental to a grooming shop. Animals pick up on that.

The end of August approached. It was slow, so the business took a much-needed vacation and closed for a week. I'd been mentally planning to meet with the manager to let him know I needed a manager and not a bather who wasn't dialed into his customers, especially new ones. At this stage, under the circumstances, I wasn't committed to this shop. Such thoughts would soon become irrelevant, anyway.

With the shop closed for a week, my mom and I took a much-needed vacation. She recently lost her husband, my step-dad Mike from cancer. I wanted out of the heat so it proved to be an almost perfect vacation. I say almost because everything was great until it was time to get back to Phoenix.

Our return flight took off forty minutes late. It began to sink in: Because of the delay, I wouldn't catch a connecting flight to Phoenix until the next day. I texted the manager as soon as this became clear. The response: "Well, you've got a full schedule tomorrow, and I'm on my hands and knees scrubbing baseboards. I've barely had any vacation and am not getting a paycheck because being closed for a week. Now I've got you telling me after nine days off that you may not return to work tomorrow. Sorry, but I need you here. So, hopefully, you can figure it out."

My reply: "If you snap-shot the schedule, I can contact all appointments and reschedule for Wednesday (a day I'm not scheduled for). There's nothing else I can do. It was today's last flight to Phoenix." I set up a makeshift phone center in the hotel lobby to reschedule my appointments. As I sat, the messages from my clients began to roll in.

Client 1: OK, that works.

Client 2: Yes, that's fine! No problem!

Client 3: Wednesday will be fine. Safe travels. See you then.

Client 4: Hi Charlie, I can't do Wednesday. I will call the shop to reschedule. Thank you, and safe travels.

This took minimal effort and time. As I read my clients' responses, I realized how easy it was to reschedule their appointments and that I could not count on Man's Best Friend's to strategically pivot when presented with a transitory dilemma.

I had never once called in sick during my time there. I covered appointments that needed covering. I came in on slow days and often waited for the phone to ring to bring in business. I'd been stuck out of town because of the weather, and the scheduling issue could be easily and still gainfully adjusted.

I realized I couldn't commit to this business any longer. This disheartened me as I thought about my compassionate clients who'd been more understanding of my situation than my boss was. I reflected on it further and decided to quit.

I went to work upon my return. Once all current appointments were checked in and accounted for, I stated to the manager, "My 8 a.m. appointments are all checked in. I can finish today and be done or finish the week and pack up Saturday." He opted for the four days' worth of business. This was beyond the standard notice he received. Most of Man's Best Friend's groomers typically either walked out or stopped showing up. I went about my day as usual, but few words passed between us. He didn't seem surprised. He didn't even try to explain himself or further inquire. I wasn't changing my mind anyway. Considering the shop's current queue didn't hold two weeks of business, the four days' notice was fair enough.

ONE-YEAR GAP AS A LITERARY SQUIRREL

Rather than run through the details, I'll just say it was summer, and you could cook fajitas on the asphalt in Phoenix. It was time to make this book happen.

I dropped from the regular radar to work on it tirelessly. To fuel my motivation, I imagined I'd been given an advance for it, and now it was my job to fulfill the obligation. I found part-time employment working one day a week at a groom shop even closer than Man's Best Friend. I delivered food. I returned to Chicago for visits as well.

Now, back to the story in progress.

The authorial hiatus was over, and I needed to work more. Led by the revenue potential and not the operative logistics, I stopped into, yes, Man's Best Friend while on errands. I was offered four temporary days filling in for a groomer who would be out of town. After I worked the four days, they offered me permanent Tuesdays and Saturdays, which would pay my rent. I wouldn't have to work the one day per week at the other grooming shop.

When the newest staff of groomers at Man's Best Friend asked why I'd left before, I'd just say I'd saved enough to take time off, travel a bit, and work on *A Chizona Résumé: Backstage on the General Labor Tour*. Plus, it wasn't like Man's Best Friend had ripped me off even though its culture hadn't been "man's best friend." I returned there and accepted how it ran.

I quickly fell back into the groove. Working Saturday mornings after playing out on Friday nights could be tough, but my dad had done it for years with a family to support. I knew I could swing it.

So, for about a year, it was almost like I'd never left. The one groomer who was there when I'd quit the first time was gone, and now there were two very likeable coworkers.

Then came Coronavirus. In November 2020, the damn Coronavirus had its stronghold over the country. We didn't fully close the shop until one of the groomers got ill, and then I got sick. I had COVID really bad, too. After we got better, we re-opened and continued working through the pandemic. We needed only the pets, so contagious contact with people seemed minimal. The other groomers weren't happy about working during COVID, however, and they further were frustrated by the usual discrepancies. One of them quit while the other was searching the job market. With just the two of us left, I told her we could deal with groomer drama and a lack of appointments elsewhere, or we could accept Man's Best Friend's unconventional ways along with a full schedule that let us sit back and count cash. My reasoning helped her decision. She managed for another year. Then one day, she packed up after-hours and simply left her key. Several groomers would later come and go. On a few occasions, I even followed teary-eyed groomers outside asking them not to quit right there and to at least finish the day (otherwise my own day would have heaped extra hell with doubled appointments).

Once again I was destined to orbit the manager's lost-in-space mindset, and the position became too much to plow through daily. All the while, along the road leading to this, everyone I knew had been telling me to open my own shop. Even the newest groomer at Man's Best Friend had asked me on the first day we worked together why I didn't have my shop. My father said he didn't want to hear any more about my job until I did something about it. The shop manager ran the business his way and, one could argue, not to industry standards. In the end, if you didn't like it, you could leave. It was my time to *vamoose*.

What would be my unexpected last day arrived. My second stint with Man's Best Friend would conclude with a verbal altercation between the manager and me punctuated by my resigning at day's end. Coincidentally, I groomed more dogs and grossed more pay that day than I ever had for a single day at the shop.

As I had once before, I left feeling liberated. I raised my hand in a Ronnie James Dio rock and roll gesture commonly known as "the fork" and texted my father: "I quit my job today!" I would be all right. I'd saved sufficient money again.

Chapter 63

Scottsdale Pet Hotel

Scottsdale, Arizona, 2018–19
- Groomer/laundry-room troll
- Total income: $2,273.00

In between stints at Man's Best Friend, I discovered nearby Scottsdale Pet Hotel. They offered one day of work per week. I had saved some money and still needed to preserve it. Grooming paid well, and working one full day each week would cover my rent.

Scottsdale Pet Hotel was a small building with many twists that turned through doors leading to play and boarding areas. I was impressed by the boarding facility's atypical cleanliness and lack of odor. If I had had a pet, I would have boarded it there.

The owner was from Illinois, which favored me. I brought in before-and-after pictures of my best grooms, and she liked what she saw. My interview was brief. I did essential grooming. Most boarding facilities required just the basics. Scottsdale Pet Hotel needed reliability more than fanciness, making us a good fit. The staff was amicable and accommodating. Everyone seemed to get along.

Unfortunately, they could offer only Fridays. I was back to having a lot of free time, so I continued writing and joined a new band—both positives.

I realized that the grooming area needed an environment more conducive to working with pets. For starters, the area was crude and located in the laundry room. The setting lent itself to many interruptions and loud banging noises that always disturbed the cat or dog being groomed. Few people closed the washer quietly. I questioned the logic of repeat returns to a washer and dryer for one or two towels. Why not just use a basket?

I was isolated in the grooming area, which I liked, but there was a lot of barking when boarding was full. Fortunately, I could close the grooming area so that pets were undisturbed. One day a week was all I could take. One drawback was that I wasn't able to interact with the pet owners at this job. I did though have my weekends free: a rarity for groomers.

This was my first 1099 position, and I was paid by check at the end of my workday. 50% commission plus tips went to me. This amount met my temporary target income. It was good to have a steady stream.

While the tips could be a bit low, the shop charged properly for the service. They likewise were proactive about charging owners for matted-down pets and large dog shave-downs. I resumed grooming cats as well.

Scottsdale Pet Hotel prioritized boarding pets over scheduling grooms. Full grooming days were rare, and my position would never grow. I didn't foresee any changes in scope. I decided to return to a job that I quit (something I never done before) so I offered Scottsdale Pet Hotel a two-week notice they deemed wasn't necessary.

I fulfilled my last day. It was a nice payday with a simple departure. It included a couple of bath-only appointments that wouldn't have otherwise been on my schedule: perhaps their way of *throwing me a bone* to wish me farewell.

Chapter 64

Nail Trim AZ

Phoenix, Arizona, 2019–present
- Self-employed groomer/trimmer of pets' nails
- Total income: Some pocket cash

All those nail trim only appointments over the years lit a bulb in my brain. An in-home nail trim service could be profitable. August 6, 2019, was my forty-fourth birthday, and I decided to hit the streets with my Razor scooter and 850 fliers. It was cloudy and a cool day to promote my business.

Placing door hangers in 2019 was markedly different from when I'd done it fifteen years before. People had become more standoffish. Nowadays, more homes have doorbell cameras too. One time, mistaken for a package thief, I attracted multiple squad cars pulling up on me to check my story.

In many other instances, barking dogs would storm the front door, further validating my business-building efforts. While placing the hangers as the dogs scratched at the doors, I'd say, "Call me—I can hear your nails!"

Whether I encountered them while handing out fliers or simply walking by them as pedestrians, people seemed interested in what I offered. Getting a dog or cat in the car can be a gaping chasm to completing a nail trim. I uploaded videos, especially those demonstrating how a nail trim can be done for an unwilling pet.

Many of my eventual clients were elderly, and I removed that challenge for them. It was a straightforward service for any pet owner and an easy one for me to provide. All I needed were a tiny bag of tools and a transport.

One day, during a visit back to Illinois, I was sitting at my dad's table, which had family pictures under a clear-vinyl table cover. One of my fliers was under it, and I noticed the phone number was misprinted. D'OH! And there I'd been, frustrated but patient and focused while waiting for the calls to begin after hanging hundreds of fliers over a year.

Professional tip: *Proofread the details forward and backward and then have someone else do the same before you print and distribute!*

Eventually I obtained the proper signage and acquired clientele. Since I was now working for myself, I could choose my uniform, and being in AZ, I went full shorts or scrub pants in the winter months. Doing a nail trim in blue jeans would have prevented the flexibility I needed. Because of its practicality, the breathable grooming smock made its way into my apparel as well.

Chapter 65

Postmates & Lyft

Phoenix, Arizona, dates mixed and overlapping
- Food and people delivery/road choont
- Total income unknown

Enter the age of twenty first–century smartphone-app jobs freeing up the stereotype claiming there is always a need for bartenders! Delivery apps have transformed unemployment for many. I discovered that most drivers drive either full-time or for supplemental income.

To maintain my savings and stay afloat, I started delivering food through Postmates. Postmates appealed to me because my car wasn't up to standards for human transport, and I didn't like the idea of driving people around. Delivering for Postmates was a bit of a sign-up process. A bank account, a smartphone, an insured vehicle, and a valid driver's license were needed to be a driver for them. I would use a separate app to track mileage and time.

Dinner deliveries were required in order to make the promoted (and best-case scenario) $22 per hour. In Phoenix, I could pull up my traffic app between 3 p.m. and 6 p.m. on any weekday and easily find three or four accidents. I did not want to drive in heavy traffic. I quickly determined that food deliveries wouldn't pay the bills. However, I had a flexible schedule and tried to utilize that by working when I wanted while avoiding stressful traffic jams.

Postmates has a simple-to-use app that dings when a delivery is available. However, I could see only the pick-up location, not the drop-off. The remaining specifics arrived after I accepted the delivery. I aimed to skirt apartment complexes, hospitals, and any drop-offs for which I'd have to leave the vehicle and travel a distance on foot. It just wasn't worth the driver's $4 share of the charge.

Cash tips were non-existent, and being tipped in the online checkout was rare. So, you might imagine the frustration of delivering at apartment complexes with many parking restrictions. Apartment-complex deliveries are both time-consuming and unsafe. Being a lone freelancer, I could disappear at such a delivery and not have it be known for some time. With restaurant-specific drivers, the operation will notice if their drivers never come back!

Postmates didn't offer the means for customers to rate their drivers. This protected the drivers from rants and complaints. Let's face it: Some American consumers can be spoiled and ready to complain about anything, even more so when they can unload simply by typing. I understood Postmates' policy. Often in the U.S., our well-intentioned drive to serve even the implacable often throws us at their mercy.

I saw a lot of disorganization with arranging pickups at restaurants. The same was true for drop-offs. At times you'd have multiple delivery drivers trying to enter and exit apartment complexes with coded security gates and limited parking.

Early on, I decided never to double-check the customer's food. I wouldn't want an unregulated driver to go through my food. If there was an issue, it was the restaurant's problem. Having food delivered involves a level of trust that I don't have. Many adults will check their kid's Halloween candy yet accept food and drink delivered by a stranger who hasn't been vetted.

I saw couples working together, which can work out well. There were certain deliveries I avoided because I would have trouble accessing them by myself. Having a runner supporting a driver can circumvent many issues. For couples, it can create a way to spend time with each other. I liked Postmates. Drivers could choose to deliver by foot, bike, or car.

In 2023, I acquired a newer vehicle. I briefly drove for Lyft after I no longer delivered for Postmates. While driving people around wasn't my favorite delivery work, it was way easier than delivering food, and their app made it convenient to manage your day. In the end, I preferred not having to exit my vehicle to deliver food; I could deal with possibly irritable human passengers. I only had to make sure I didn't drink too much coffee!

I wasn't making a lot of money because I wanted to avoid driving around Phoenix during rush hour, which seemed to be a common denominator for these driver by app jobs. I did have opportunities to introduce myself to many pet owners and market my budding independent business, Nail Trim AZ.

After a couple years of scrub pants and grooming smocks, it was nice to come back to casual with a pair of possibly faded blue jeans, shorts, heavy metal t-shirts, or any other relaxed attire I wanted.

Puzzle Rides

Scottsdale/Prescott, Arizona, 2023–25

- Puzzlemaster/comedian/tour-leading sensei
- Total income: Approximately $20,000.00 and counting

In May 2023, I had been looking at locations for my own groom shop. I saw a post looking for puzzle masters on a Facebook page I follow called "Comedy Open Mics in Phx. & The Valley." Yes, that's right: puzzle master!

The post asked, "Are you looking for a job to showcase your jokes? Try it on one of our golf carts while giving puzzle rides!" The ad requested that applicants private-message the inbox. This was one of the easiest application processes I had ever done. I followed instructions by messaging the inbox directly with my name and phone number. Applying for a job has gotten easy folks.

I was called in for an interview where they kept golf carts. It was a cool, enjoyable concept I connected with right away. Puzzle Rides is a one-of-a-kind mobile–escape room style clue finding experience on golf carts solving your way to different points of interests throughout

Old Town Scottsdale or Prescott. I could tell on my first ride that I would make this job work. Interacting with customers was second nature to me.

Puzzle Rides thanked me for following the application process properly, which proved to be a public challenge. Others failed by typing the word "interested" in the comments of the job posting. I don't know what reality applicants linger in if they think employers come to them. I feel employers could avoid this headache by turning off the ability to comment, but then how would they filter out those who cannot follow simple instructions? They offered me the job of puzzle master, I jokingly responded, "hmm, interested."

Escape rooms were new to me. To prepare, I did an escape room with my family. It was fun, and it helped me understand what I was getting into.

Summer in Phoenix is too hot for puzzle rides, so my training rides were limited to occasional early morning and evenings. It was a lot to grasp at once—almost overwhelming. I quickly noticed how involved and thought-out the rides were. The job was more than just driving a golf cart. To succeed, drivers needed a flexible schedule and the ability to plan.

I didn't realize how much there would be to absorb in a short time. Going on a few rides with customers was the best way to learn. For additional practice I waited until it was late in Old Town Scottsdale and then drove the routes in my car. I would have preferred to bike it, but the nighttime temperatures could still be in the low 100s! Learning about Old Town Scottsdale as I explored it was fun, and I got to share that knowledge with my riders.

After I participated in a few more training rides that involved driving the cart and mastering the game kits, they felt comfortable giving me codes and combinations to access the golf carts and supply chests. Being a puzzle master is 100% self-management, which I immediately understood.

The game kits were secured with combination padlocks and other locking gadgets that had to be mastered before we could host riders. The game kits were to be locked back up properly so they were ready for another ride. One tricky part was correctly repacking the game kits: It had to be perfect. Each game was in a set order corresponding to the different puzzle-ride stops. Each stop on the route had a lock to solve that would then get the group to the next location. I had to know the specific routes Puzzle Rides used to play the game.

My valet experience proved to support the finer points of being a puzzle master. As a valet must, a puzzle master has to remember many things, and mistakes can be costly. Encountering the general public who are not necessarily customers while on rides was a similar dynamic.

The golf carts had an extensive check-in and check-out procedure. It was simple, but there was no room for error. The carts had to be returned to the precise rented spaces.

Old Town Scottsdale is broken up by little side streets that run on angles along the Arizona Canal. I routed each themed ride on paper pocket maps to use as cheat sheets until I knew the routes to which I taped an index card detailing the ride's combinations, such as for toy ciphers, luggage locks, and puzzle pods.

There are solo rides with one cart or up to twenty riders in multiple carts. Each ride began with checking the app to ensure all riders' waivers were signed. Once the ride began and we rolled out of the parking lot, I could get social while working on the game.

This was another 1099 position, meaning I'd handle my own taxes and invoicing. The position required a smartphone and the ability to download the scheduling software. I found a free invoicing app I could use to track my rides. Bottom line: It wasn't an hourly position you simply clocked in for and then did as you were told. You were paid per ride plus tips. Plus, with sufficient notice, for nights when I was to play music, I could take that whole day off.

Looking back on it, in the beginning, I took the job for granted. I focused more on the fun than the details and had to remind myself to be alert to golf-cart safety. Getting careless while driving could be easy, particularly with a multi-cart race. My attention to certain specifics could sometimes slip, even as one who seeks to apply method and analysis for understanding and efficiency.

I needed to be my typically more-diligent self. I made a daily checklist on a notecard with customer info and reminders. My cheat-sheet maps were handy too. I wanted to do the job well and put my heart into it. I knew that in time I'd get to be myself as I continued settling into the role. I saw even more clearly its potential as the easy, likable, good-paying job I thought it could be.

From tourists to locals, I encountered different people daily. All of them wanted to talk and have a good time. I couldn't imagine a better way to socialize. I could run and adapt each game according to the particular group. For example, a ride might include families, friends, teenage groups, coworkers, or a mix of them all. Some were more participative and social than others. Along the way I found that even a grumpy teenager could be inspired to embrace the game. I used puns and pop culture references to clue riders properly through the game without lessening the experience. As my skills progressed, Puzzle Rides soon started booking up my day.

The tips I got were excellent and helpful to my living-based revenue. As with grooming pets and parking cars, for every person who doesn't tip, someone else does, often generously. Most people were very good tippers, especially if you engaged them with spirit, humor and linked them to photos from the ride afterward.

Keeping kids involved in activities is my jam. Getting them through the puzzle ride while having fun and giving parents ways to take mental breaks for an hour inspired many tips. Kids are easy to have fun with; they're always ready for it. Just treat them with the same good nature and will as you would an adult.

My schedule varied from week to week and sometimes day to day. I would occasionally have days with a large gap between rides. Some puzzle masters may have found that too long of a day. My flexible availability made me reliable for Puzzle Rides.

The following summer had record heat starting June 1st at 110 degrees for fifty-eight straight days. Puzzle Rides couldn't operate in that heat. The time off from work finally allowed me to have foot surgery requiring four to six weeks off my feet.

I was set to have my surgery when another load of life's bricks dropped. I was at a baseball game when I learned that LLF Sam Cinquegrani had passed away in his sleep. Ugh. I had spoken with him days earlier. He was advising me on a laptop purchase. This news hit hard. Between having surgery and feeling Sam's departure, my timely break from Puzzle Rides came right on cue.

Sam's close friends and I honored him a few months later by spending what would have been his 50th birthday with our beloved Mrs. C. (Chapter 8), and Sam's immediate family. Losing people sucks.

When the summer finally let up I was back to puzzlemastering. Pain free working after years of foot aches! By the following summer I started doing rides up in Prescott, chasing the Arizona dream to have a cooler place to work in the summer. I could see myself repeating the process each year. At the same time, growth was slow, and puzzle masters were hard to keep, so simply remaining Puzzle Master Charlie was fine with me. It was an easy job where I could network while making good money. Where some past employees could not last, I wasn't letting lack of growth keep me from doing my job and serving so many good-natured people.

Work attire for this job was simple. Some puzzle masters wore blue jeans, and the job was casual enough for some untattered blue jeans. I found golf pants in the winter to early spring months to be perfect. They breathe and stretch, making them very comfortable. Once it warmed up, it was all solid-color shorts. Puzzle Rides had simple black t-shirts with the company logo printed on the front for us to wear.

On occasion, I'd adorn a cowboy hat for your Wild West Heist, a viper bandana on your Pirate Treasure Adventure, or skull mask on one of our Ghost Riders. My blue-jean attitude had evolved since moving to the desert, where I found blue jeans to be suitable mainly for when I went out at night.

Puzzle Rides deserved both happiness and success. They created a unique business concept that sells fun. The owners were big Star Wars fans too. If you're a fan, you probably know what Order 66 is. (chapter heading). Each day, I learned to improve the puzzle rides. Most important to me, my people skills remained on the whetting stone. I can think of few better ways to keep those skills refined than by addressing different groups several times daily.

Being puzzle-master took me all the way through the challenging but necessary final stages to get this book published. I enjoyed working for Puzzle Rides, serving others with fresh ears for jokes. I often looked back at riders asking, "Do you believe they pay me for this?"

As we approach the publishing date for this book, I've mentally moved closer to becoming an author. And that, folks, can be a chapter of its own!

Chapter 67

Published Author

A Chizona Résumé: Backstage on the General Labor Tour.

Planet Earth, 2010–present
- Self-proclaimed writer/retiree/celebrator

In 2023, I moved out of south Scottsdale and in with my girlfriend, Angela. She has been a wonderful person and a true companion in this life story of mine. She has supported this book and its progress from the moment I mentioned it to her. Together, we sufficiently manage and meet our expenses. It's her nicer vehicle I used to work for LYFT.

This book has been more than a decade in the making. I have referred to it often as a topic- starter when talking with others. The idea to write it arrived while I was sitting in an airport returning from training in Colorado for my position with Aussie Mobile Pet (Chapter 41). Hoping it would be the last time I took a new job, I started thinking about how many jobs I had along the way. I started making a list, and as it grew, I thought, "Wow, that has to be a record." Seeing the thickening number, I kept that list, and as I continued to update it, it began to resemble a table of contents. When I tell people about writing a book based on my resume, it typically pushes their laugh button. At a certain point, I had to decide how all my job experiences would translate into my particular life journey.

I am truly grateful for the support I've received as I've written this book. We all appreciate extra flickering candles when we're making our way through the tunnels of a long-term endeavor. I am grateful for the lifelong friendship I have with my editor Jon Davis whose vision and familiarity with my voice helped me craft a readable product.

Real research went into writing this as well: dates, chronology, names of people and businesses that had faded into the mist of the past. A report from the Social Security Administration showed me my gross earnings and helped me correct any mistakes regarding dates. I like numbers and facts. They can frequently offer truth.

I've solidified the vital practice of constantly saving work done on computers. I save mine on two separate flash drives before each break and periodically throughout my current writing session.

I have enjoyed writing my story, and as the saying goes, it ain't over yet. I find fulfillment and solace just typing away. Phoenix weather is so lovely that I can leave my door and windows open for fresh air to flow in as I think and create. Sometimes I pause to put seeds out for the wild birds that flutter down to keep me company.

While managing the valet stand for American Valet (Chapter 57), I started reading *Ghost Rider: Travels on the Healing Road* by the late Neil Peart, my favorite drummer and lyricist of Rush. I laughed and cried while reading it. Rush is my "deserted-island band," meaning if I was dropped on an empty island with only one music catalog to listen to, it would be Rush. In 1997, Neil Peart lost his daughter in a tragic car accident after leaving their home on the way back to school. Less than a year later, his wife died from cancer, or in his view, a heart broken by loss.

Neil Peart was an excellent writer whether composing a book or a song. The Rush albums he wrote lyrics for were stories, so he could easily chronicle his 55,000-mile motorcycle journey across North and Central America. His book opened my eyes to how to report to the reader. After twenty-five years of heavy listening to "the Holy Trio" (Rush), I was influenced by Neil Peart again. *Ghost Rider* had represented his transition from lyricist to author, a pursuit he continued after his inaugural effort. As he had with drums, he went all in as a long-form writer, determined to explore with honesty, perception, and detail his life's observations, revelations, and imaginings. His conviction to leave those meaningful accounts for the rest of us to reflect on fanned the flames of my own. After losing my brother, my stepdad, my cousin, and close friends, I could relate to loss in this world.

I read autobiographies by Eric Clapton, Duff McKagan, Sammy Hagar, Rodney Dangerfield, Willie Nelson, Ernest Borgnine, Jacob Slichter, Peter Criss, Eddie Johnson, Dave Mustaine, Mötley Crüe, Matt Groening, and Steven Tyler. These stories shared realistic, common themes of personal loss, everyday relations, and hardships that don't go away with success; these are still people who can hurt just as easily as we do. Sometimes, they might hurt even easier because their lives are exposed to complete strangers with no connection to the human behind the public persona. This can give pain an unfair extra advantage. Another thing each story relays is that it is not a distant world away. We too can pursue and enjoy our own kind of success when we remain realistic about our life and circumstances.

As I have gone through this process of writing a book, I've found many others claiming to be doing the same, just like playing drums. Whenever I tell someone that I'm a drummer, many may say something like "So am I! My parents bought me a Mickey Mouse drum set for Christmas!"

It becomes clearer to me that a lot of us want to create something and give it to the world—something that proves that we're here—even if it's just the dog that is paying attention. We want to express what is felt and shaped in us as we pass through the adventure.

I find that I don't want the book to end because the time I spend writing it feels so meaningfully productive. Perhaps my accountings along the general laborpalooza tour will evolve into a book tour of its own.

Writing is more than fun: It gives me purpose as well. I look forward to doing it again.

EPILOGUE

I firmly believe that anything I've recorded here reinforces the messages that I've intended. I recognize my story's subjectivity. Although for me many of these jobs were extraordinary in their choontiness, I know people throughout America deal with similar situations all the time. My wish is that in sharing my own, I offer the amusing familiarity of following the script as it's being written for us with the cosmos' sardonic sense of humor.

While most of us will not be destined to be celebrities or members of the 1%, we are still a society where our independence can and will lead to good things if we are focused, honest, and persistent in our efforts. The ordinary worker who feels they have nothing to offer or strive for needs only to adjust their personal lens. I can think of few people who enjoy job searching and navigating repetitive, boring, non-creative labor and problematic personalities for a pittance of a paycheck. For some, it's simpler to work a crappy job that's familiar over a job search for a new uncharted one.

We all need to work. We all need a job that helps us pay to live. But if our place of employment makes us miserable getting up in the morning and equally so just getting through the day, at some point we have to take inventory of our time on this earth. As I move further into middle age, I recognize just how finite and unpromised that time is. Unlike money, it is a resource that cannot be replenished. If your priorities allow and your responsibilities are in order, save money, keep that résumé updated, tie up loose ends, aim for greater frugality, and be prepared for the old Costanza walkout. When it is called for, freedom is a powerful, cleansing human sensation. Until then, don't lay yourself on the rack for those to whom you're a commodity in the end. Take time off to recharge, even if it's not PTO (paid time off). If you do have PTO, for crying out loud, use it—all of it! Call in sick even if you're not. Leave early if you can. Life really is too short to spend it strictly in the grind.

If I'm to leave you with one thing after all of this, it's that the concept of success for the everyday person is not what high-profile American image and culture might have us believe—because let's face it, almost all of us at some point might imagine the good life equates to respect, recognized status, and comfortable financial freedom. Sometimes things play out a certain way in one's life to indicate with every pointer that they just aren't made for the system we've built for "stable" employment. Some people just don't fit, even when they try. I'm one of those.

Many of us will move from job to job in this life, doing what we must, paying the bills, working for others. Many of us will do it with only a fleeting sense of happiness. We know something isn't quite right; something is missing. Plus, to turn the screw further, stacking jobs on a résumé can block us from being a job candidate because of employers' fear we can't commit. For example, while living in Nevada, I interviewed for a porter position at a motorcycle dealership that I was excited for. It came down to me and another. The manager even called me back in for a follow-up interview to meet the owner. He later explained that he gave the job to the other applicant because my job history had too many entries. My awareness awakened: Potential employers and I would often thump different drums between what they thought they wanted and what I was searching for. I began to tailor my résumé to the job I was applying for and included only relevant experience.

It's possible at times I give the impression of being a sarcastic malcontent who holds the world to account for jobs not working out. The truth lies in the middle, between the jobs and me. Because I was not a natural thread in the quilt, I could do little but fray it. In the end, I'm probably better off without many of those jobs, and they—even with some of my efficiencies—were unlikely to receive all they wanted from me.

Success in the end, at least to me, is the completion of any task you have set out to achieve. It starts in our heart, takes form in our mind, and comes to life through our actions. It is finding a way to gather the ups and the downs, the good times and the misadventures, and the wisdom both serenely and painfully gained and then carry it forward so that our story might inspire others and remind them they are not alone.

And so with that, I say good luck. May your purpose grow in your vision and make your own special story—because it is special.

That, and may your path wind you away from choonts as you go.

Acknowledgments

Al & Eunice "Rustie" Sochacki, Mike & Robbie Howe-Sherrill.

Angela Wood

Adam, Anne Marie, Jackie, and Angelina Turner. Greg, Lucas, and Logan Turner. Fred, Ava, and Freddie Sochacki. Teresa Sochacki and Trent Seigler. Janice, Nathan, Mila, and Deacon Varnagatas. Shelina & Jen Seigler-Mandela.

Marty & Jackie Church, Mark Jordan, Tim Jordan, Hal & Lori Turner. Beth Adams-Russel. David Bon. Denise Kanne. Sam Cinquegrani. Charlie Cinquegrani, Jon Davis, Laura Coleman. "Lefty" Dave Hernandez. Jeff & Laura Lee. Erika Medinger. Bob Medinger.

Dr. Rob Dann. Dr. Sheldon Rubin. Jeff Mcclusky. Arnie Luczak. Neil Peart & RUSH.

Brandy, Zoe and Janosh Sochacki. Gus Sochacki (my Lil brudder), Tigger Wood "TIggs", Trek Seigler and Tater Mandela, Sadie, Sunny and Talia Varnagatas. Cooper Turner, Milo Turner, Mojo Bon, Smeagol Sochacki, Vera Turner-Sochacki, Lucky and Strike Coleman. And Buster.

Coming Soon

30 bands in 30 years: A Chizona on Drums Entertainment Resume

Next Up

You've got the book, now get the full experience by visiting my website, **Chizona.com**, where you'll find exclusive content not available elsewhere.